# honey we're killing the kids

## the ten rules for healthy and happy children

## Kristina Murrin

BBC ACTIVE

This book is published to accompany the television series, *Honey We're Killing the Kids*, first transmitted in 2005.
Executive Producer: Robin Ashbrook
Producer: Dympna Jackson
Production Manager: Elisabeth Bayliffe

Educational Publishers LLP trading as BBC Active
Edinburgh Gate
Harlow
Essex CM20 2JE
England

First published 2006

ISBN 0 563 52007 8

Commissioned by Emma Shackleton
Project Edited by Helena Caldon
Designed by Annette Peppis
Commissioned photographs by Chris Capstick © BBC Active
Production Controller: Man Fai Lau

Printed and bound by Bath Press Ltd

The Publisher's policy is to use paper manufactured from sustainable forests.

# Contents

# Introduction

Children misbehave. It's a fact of life. But how you deal with bad behaviour can make a huge difference to your child – both in the short term and later in life. Some parents let their children run riot; others are so strict that the child never really has a chance to just 'be a child'. So where's the happy balance?

Parenting has never been easy, but mums and dads of this generation seem to be having a particularly hard time. Not only are there an unprecedented amount of things to worry about – from violent crime to computer games – but there also seems to be very little agreement about what's best for our children. Ask two different 'experts' and you'll get two different replies – whether the topic is working mums or what to do about obese children. As a parent this lack of consensus can be very confusing.

On top of this, no-one ever gets taught how to be a parent. It seems crazy that in order to drive a car you need to have lessons and pass a test, but that parents get very little support or guidance about the most important job in the world – bringing up children. What information we do get has to be gleaned from friends, relatives, the media and other parents; much of which is often out-of-date or unhelpful. It's no wonder that levels of obesity, sleep deprivation, teenage pregnancy and other childhood problems have reached an all-time high.

That's one of the reasons I was so keen to make *Honey We're Killing the Kids*. Rather than try to push a particular agenda or give you my own brand of parenting (and let's face it, as a mother of three I'm still learning), I've tried to sort the facts from the fiction when it comes to the issues surrounding parenting. I wanted to answer some of the common questions parents ask, such as, 'What constitutes a healthy diet?' or, 'How much exercise does my child need?' by digging out facts based on the best available science and research. Then, as a parent, you can go away and decide what to do with this knowledge. After all, you know your children better than anyone.

What also makes *Honey We're Killing the Kids* so different from other parenting programmes is the breadth of children's issues we tackle. As you'll see in the following chapters we look at diet, exercise, sleep, learning, love, getting involved, discipline, respect, safety and good communication. We know that there are certain factors that influence how long our children will live and how happy they'll be throughout their lifetimes – diet and exercise play a big part in this – but there also are some other factors you might not have thought of, such as how sociable your children are or how much sleep they get. As you will have seen on the series, even the smallest changes in these areas can have immediate and long-lasting benefits for the whole family.

I have great admiration for all the families who took part in the series. I'm not sure I would have had the courage to open the door to a camera crew and have my parenting skills questioned on prime-time television! Yes, we had tears, real heartfelt shock and a huge amount of guilt, but at the end of the day none of the parents featured in the series were bad parents; they were just people who loved their children dearly but hadn't made the connection between their parenting style and its implications for the future.

When we showed parents where their children were heading it was always a nasty surprise, but it was also a huge motivation for them to alter their lifestyles. Most of the families had an initial struggle with the rules because

'Parents are role models: your children look to you to show them how the world works and how to behave in it, and they copy what you do.'

I was asking them to make such fundamental changes, but all of the parents knew what was at stake and therefore how important it was to make these changes. Best of all, without exception, each family said it was actually easier and quicker to make positive changes than they ever thought it would be.

I'm really hoping that this book inspires you to adopt some of the simple principles and advice from the programme and start adapting it to your own family. When it comes down to it, parents are role models: your children look to you to show them how the world works and how to behave in it, and they copy what you do. That's a great responsibility, but it's also a fantastic opportunity to bring the best out in your child. It's your job to teach them about life and guide them towards lifelong health, happiness and personal fulfilment. Good parenting starts with you.

# 1

# Diet

A healthy diet is one of the most important gifts you can give your child. Not only is good food vital for optimum health, but children also need a wholesome diet to help them grow and develop. We all want what's best for our children, so why are we letting them eat such junk?

## How healthy are your children's diets?

**Unfortunately, a large proportion of young people don't eat balanced meals – only one in seven children in the UK has the recommended five portions of fruit and veg per day, while one in five is classed as obese. Today's children also consume twice as much salt as is healthy and put away an alarming average of half a kilo of sugary food per day.**

## Unhealthy diet, unhealthy children

Deceptively, whatever their diet, children often seem to have boundless energy and good health. However, children who eat huge amounts of processed food, snacks, sweets and fizzy drinks might look healthy on the outside, but what's going on inside their bodies is very different.

The main risk from a diet high in fat, sugar and salt is obesity. The proportion of children in the UK who are overweight or obese rose sharply in the 1980s and has continued to climb at a worrying rate. According to World Health Organization figures, the amount of British children aged between two and four who are obese nearly doubled between 1989 and 1998. For those aged between six and 15, obesity rates grew even faster; trebling from five per cent to 16 per cent between 1990 and 2001 – that's almost one in every five children. And mums and dads are no better; the same study found that, overall, 52 per cent of mothers and 72 per cent of fathers were either overweight or obese.

## Does it matter if your child is overweight?

Surely a little bit of 'puppy fat' is nothing to worry about in children? And haven't we got enough things to worry about on top of trying to keep our youngsters from scoffing junk food? Well, yes and no. While children need to feel loved and accepted for who they are and not what they look like, letting your child become overweight is not doing them any favours in the long term. Most children who are obese infants become obese adults – they never develop healthy eating habits. While obsessing about body image isn't, admittedly, healthy for a child, teaching your children about good food is a vital tool that they should take through into adulthood.

Obesity is tough for a child: someone who is overweight in childhood is twice as likely to die from heart disease when they reach adulthood, and fat children who become fat adults are more likely to suffer from high blood pressure and certain types of cancer.

But obesity in childhood can also have an effect on the here and now. The significant increase in numbers of children with diabetes has been largely attributed to rising levels of obesity, and fat children are also more likely to have sleep disorders and psychological problems, such as low self-esteem.

Not every child who eats badly is obese, but that doesn't mean that they won't be at risk from health problems. A child who is thin but eats a high-fat diet can still have an increased cholesterol level – which is a risk factor in heart disease. A diet that is deficient in vitamins A, C and E (the ones you get from fruit, veg and wholemeal bread), increases your child's risk of cancer and heart problems. Equally, too much salt can lead to raised blood pressure, which puts you at greater risk for heart attacks and strokes. The wrong diet can also affect the functioning of the major organs, can lower our immunity, and has been shown to encourage behavioural problems such as poor concentration and hyperactivity.

So, in fact, poor nutrition is responsible for adversely affecting many different areas of a child's mental and physical health and is thought to contribute to:

* Poor concentration.
* Mood swings and hyperactivity.
* Food cravings.
* Communication problems.
* Tiredness and irritability.
* Panic attacks and anxiety.
* Asthma and other allergies.
* Sleep problems.
* Learning difficulties.

On the other hand, research shows that a good diet helps a child to maintain a healthy weight, improves physical growth and protects against life-threatening illnesses such as heart disease and some cancers. A good diet also has a positive effect on behaviour – it can help your child to do better academically by improving concentration and general behaviour. It will even give them more energy during the day and help them to sleep better at night.

## What children should be eating

It can be tough being a parent, especially when it comes to what you should feed your children. One minute we're told that children need lots of calcium from milk, for example, the next we're told to watch out for dairy allergies. It's the same with all sorts of foods and in recent years the number of food scares, such as salmonella, BSE, GM and pesticides, have exhausted parents to the point of utter confusion. So what should children really be eating?

For years now we have understood the basics of a healthy diet. *Whether you are an adult or a child the advice is the same*: a balanced diet should contain a variety of food types, including:

*   At least five portions of fruit and veg a day.
*   Non-refined starchy foods, such as wholemeal bread and wholegrain cereals.
*   Some protein-rich foods, such as meat, fish, eggs and lentils.
*   Some dairy foods.

It's also important that food is freshly made and not processed because ready meals and junk food use lots of preservatives, have low vitamin and mineral levels and are high in fat and salt. (Fat and salt are cheap ways to make bland processed food taste better.)

### Fruit and veg

If there's one thing that's key to you and your family's dietary health it's eating five portions of fruit and veg a day. At the moment the average fruit and vegetable consumption in England is less than three portions a day, and yet increasing this quantity is the quickest way to help reduce the risk of some cancers and protect against heart disease. What's more, fruit and veg taste great and add variety to any meal. Eating five portions a day

## Count to five

**What counts as one portion of fruit or veg?**

**Green vegetables:** 2 broccoli spears, 8 cauliflower florets, 4 heaped tablespoons of cabbage or green beans.

**Cooked vegetables:** 3 heaped tablespoons, such as carrots, peas or sweetcorn.

**Salad vegetables:** 3 sticks of celery, 2-inch cube of cucumber, 1 medium tomato, 7 cherry tomatoes.

**Tinned/frozen vegetables:** 3 heaped tablespoons of tinned or frozen carrots, peas or sweetcorn.

**Pulses and beans:** 3 heaped tablespoons of kidney, cannellini or butter beans, or chick peas (beans or pulses can only count as one of your five-a-day portions).

**Fresh fruit:** 1 medium-sized fruit, such as 1 apple, banana, pear or orange.

**Small-sized fruit:** 2 plums, 2 satsumas, 2 kiwi fruit, 3 apricots, 7 strawberries, 14 cherries.

**Large fruit:** ½ grapefruit, 1 slice of melon (2-inch slice), 1 large slice of pineapple, 2 slices of mango (2-inch slice).

**Dried fruit:** 1 tablespoon of raisins, currants, sultanas, mixed fruit, 2 figs, 3 prunes.

**Tinned fruit:** 2 pear or peach halves, 6 apricot halves, 8 segments of tinned grapefruit.

**Juice:** 1 medium glass (150ml) of 100 per cent fruit juice (juice only counts as one a day, no matter how much you drink).

Source: The Department of Health

might sound a lot, but it's actually much easier than you think, especially when you see what counts as one portion (see opposite).

## Starchy foods

Starchy foods are also an important part of a healthy diet. While you don't have to have them at every meal, current Government guidelines suggest that starchy foods should make up about a third of the food that we eat overall. This is because they are a great source of energy and one of the main ways in which we get vital nutrients such as fibre, calcium, iron and some essential B vitamins.

In recent years, though, starchy foods have become unfashionable. Many weight-loss diets encourage us to avoid foods such as bread, but the reality is that they contain less than half the calories of fat. The problem arises when we add fat to our starchy foods – piling lots of butter on a jacket potato or adding margarine to toast – or when we eat only refined starchy foods such as white bread or white pasta.

The healthiest types of starchy food are the wholegrain options. White or refined starchy foods have had many of the important nutrients and fibre removed and should be avoided. Wholegrain foods, on the other hand, contain lots of fibre, which is vital for healthy digestion and for preventing bowel diseases. It also takes us longer to digest wholegrain foods, which means we are less likely to suffer from hunger pangs between meals. This is especially important for children who tend to snack on junk food when they are feeling peckish.

## Healthy starchy foods

* Wholemeal, wholegrain and granary bread.
* Wholemeal pittas and chapattis.
* Wholewheat pasta.
* Brown rice.
* Wholegrain breakfast cereals.

## Protein-rich foods

We all need to eat protein-rich foods. Protein is vital because it helps the body to repair itself, and it's doubly vital for children because protein also helps the body grow and develop. Lots of foods contain protein, including chicken, lean meat, fish, eggs and dairy products, and we should be aiming to get about 15 per cent of the calories we eat from these types of foods. Oily fish (such as salmon, mackerel and sardines) is an especially good source of protein as it contains lots of other beneficial nutrients including Omega-3 fatty acids, which help keep our hearts healthy*. If you or your child is a vegetarian and these foods are not an option, don't worry because tofu, pulses and bread are also good sources of protein.

As a rough guide, men need about 50g and women need about 40g of protein a day. Children aged four to six need about 20g while those aged seven to ten need about 28g.

*Children should avoid eating any shark, swordfish or marlin. High levels of mercury in these fish can affect the development of the nervous system.

## Good protein sources

**The average child needs between 20g and 28g of protein per day, depending on their age. This equates to the following:**

* **1 chicken breast.**
* **1 portion of lean Bolognese sauce.**
* **1 small can of tuna, or 1 poached cod fillet.**
* **1 cheese sandwich in wholemeal bread.**
* **4–5 glasses of milk.**
* **6 tablespoons of boiled red lentils.**
* **1 serving of tofu.**
* **6–9 slices of wholemeal bread.**

## Dairy foods

Milk and other dairy products are a vital source of calcium, the mineral needed for your children to develop healthy bones and teeth. (A diet low in calcium can lead to osteoporosis.) Calcium is also important for muscle contraction, regulation of the heartbeat and the formation of blood clots. Dairy products are also a vital source of protein and vitamins A, B12, and D.

If your child is allergic to cows' milk or has a lactose intolerance, it's very important for them to receive sufficient calcium from other foods. Tofu, tinned fish and green leafy vegetables are good sources, and there are also a number of products on the market now that have, added calcium, such as orange juice and fortified cereals.

### Milk

After weaning, children under two should drink only whole milk because they may not get enough calories from semi-skimmed milk. From two, semi-skimmed is fine, but skimmed milk is best avoided as it is very low in calories and contains only minute amounts of vitamins A and D. As a general guide, children between one and three need about 350mg of calcium a day – two glasses of full-fat milk will give them this.

### Dairy foods and fat

While milk and dairy products are vital for children and adults, they also tend to contain a high percentage of fat. Although a certain amount of fat is essential for good health (see pages 22–3), it's important to limit your intake. Most children in the UK eat too much fat, so rather than cutting out dairy products – which contain other essential vitamins and nutrients – why not look for lower-fat versions of foodstuffs?

## Healthy dairy options for children

* Semi-skimmed milk for children over two years of age.
* Low-fat spread instead of butter.
* Cottage cheese, low-fat cream cheese, reduced-fat hard cheese.
* Low-fat fromage frais.
* Low-fat yoghurt.

## Vitamins, minerals and vegetarians

Research has shown that young people in Scotland, and to a lesser extent in northern England, tend to have lower intakes of most vitamins and minerals than they need. This is also true of children from poorer backgrounds. Our bodies need minute amounts of vitamins and minerals in order to function properly, and although the good news is that the majority of children and young people do receive adequate vitamins and minerals, a recent national survey found that there were a few notable exceptions:

* Older teenagers tend not to get enough vitamin A.
* More than a third of 11 to 14-year-old girls aren't getting enough zinc from their diet.
* Almost half of 11 to 14-year-old girls don't get enough iron.

# What vitamins and minerals do for your body

## Vitamin A

Found in animal and vegetable sources. Helps to keep bones and teeth healthy. Also maintains good vision and promotes healthy skin. If you eat enough of these foods you can build an excellent immune system which not only fights illnesses, but helps you recover from them as well.

### Food sources

Apples, bananas, blackberries, blueberries, broccoli, cabbage, carrots, corn, grapes, green beans, kiwi, leeks, lettuce, nectarines, mangoes, oranges, parsley, passion fruit, peaches, pears, peas, peppers, pink grapefruits, plums, pumpkins, raspberries, sprouts, squash, strawberries, sweet potatoes, tomatoes, watercress.

## Vitamin B

Responsible for providing energy to the body when it attempts to convert sugars found in carbohydrate foods. Consuming enough B vitamins may help relieve some conditions affected by nerves such as irritability, depression and anxiety. The natural colourants in green vegetables can actually protect the eyes against cataracts, and protect the body from toxic substances that may cause infections. These foods also contain antioxidants.

### Food sources

Brewer's yeast, brown rice, butter, cheese, eggs, fish, green veg, legumes, liver, meat, milk, peanuts, peas, potatoes, poultry, soya beans, wheat germ, wholegrain products.

## Vitamin C

Needed for growth, healing of wounds and maintenance of bones and teeth. Pink grapefruits are excellent in preventing cancers of the lung, bladder, cervix and skin. The increased amount of lycopene in foods rich in vitamin C, such as tomatoes and grapefruits, can prevent bad sunburns and protect the skin.

### Food sources

Apples, apricots, avocado, bananas, blueberries, broccoli, Brussels sprouts, cabbage, carrots, cauliflower, celery, corn, cranberries, cucumber, fennel, garlic, grapefruit, grapes, green beans, kiwi, leeks, lemons, lettuce, liver, melon, mushrooms, onions, oranges, papaya, parsley, pears, peas, pineapples, plums, potatoes, raspberries, spinach, strawberries, sweet potato, tomatoes.

## Zinc

Zinc aids food digestion, wound healing and physical growth. Eating foods containing zinc can help smell and taste functions, maintain a healthy metabolism and weight control and supports healthy growth.

**Food sources**

Beans, dairy products, fortified breakfast cereals, green vegetables, lettuce, mushrooms, nuts oysters, poultry, red meat, seafood, spinach, wholegrains.

## Iron

Used to produce red blood cells in the body and usually comes from meat, cereal and pulses. Iron helps increase the body's red blood cell count and this in turn gives more energy and helps us exercise effectively and with vigour.

**Food sources**

Broccoli, Brussels sprouts, eggs, garden peas, red meat (lamb, beef, pork), salmon, sardines, spinach, wholegrain cereals, wholemeal bread.

## Potassium

Usually found in plant-rich foods. Helps with muscle building, strength and functions of the nerves. Non-processed potassium-rich foods are best. Also, potatoes eaten with the skins are more packed with potassium than without. When eaten on a regular basis, potassium may also help prevent weight gain and control water retention in the body.

**Food sources**

Apples, apricots, bananas, cherries, coconuts, dates, grapefruits, grapes, lemons, mangoes, melon, oranges, papaya, peaches, pineapple, raisins, raspberries, strawberries, tangerines.

Vegetarians also have to be careful that they are receiving an adequate intake of vitamins and minerals. Many children, especially teenagers, choose to eat a meat-free diet, so you need to ensure their meals are balanced and include all the necessary nutrients for growth and development. Give them foods such as milk, cheese and eggs so that their diet won't be too bulky and they'll get plenty of protein, vitamin A, calcium and zinc. Iron, which is often the nutrient most deficient in a meat-free diet, is also found in many vegetables and pulses (beans, lentils and chick-peas), in dried fruit (such as apricots, raisins and sultanas) and in some breakfast cereals.

A healthy balanced diet – whether vegetarian or not – should always include a variety of vitamins and minerals. If you are eating well, you shouldn't need to boost your diet with vitamin supplements. The following chart helps you identify which are the key vitamins and minerals, why they are essential for children, and which foods contain a good supply:

## What children are really eating

Ok, we know what children should eat, but most parents will tell you the reality is very different.

It might be difficult to believe, but children actually ate more healthily in the 1950s than they do now. Research from University College London and the Medical Research Council found that despite food shortages in the post-war period, children in the fifties actually had a better intake of several key nutrients, including fibre, calcium, vitamins and iron, than they do now. This was because these children ate more bread and milk (increasing their fibre and calcium intake), drank fewer soft drinks (which meant less refined sugar), got lots of vitamin C from fresh vegetables and ate more red meat (giving them more iron).

### So what are our children eating?

In comparison, modern children are missing out. Research shows that the foods most commonly consumed by youngsters in the UK are white bread, savoury snacks, crisps, biscuits, potatoes and chocolate. One in three people also eat a ready meal more than once a week (this compares to only one in six in France). The problem with such a diet is that not only will a child who stuffs themselves on processed food and snacks be less likely to have room for fruit and vegetables, but they will also be consuming large amounts of fat, sugar and salt. A palate cultivated on artificially-flavoured foods will find it difficult to adapt to the subtler tastes of fresh, healthy produce.

> **Did you know?**
>
> One in five children eat no fruit in a week, and three in five eat no leafy green vegetables

Source: National Diet and Nutrition Survey 2000

### The main offenders
#### Fat

Fat has a bad reputation. While a diet too high in fat can lead to specific health problems, a certain amount of fat in our diet keeps us healthy. The key to a balanced diet is knowing exactly how much fat you can safely consume and recognizing the difference between the various types of fats. Fat can be divided into two groups: saturated and unsaturated.

## Saturated fats

These usually come from animal sources and are found in foods such as butter, cheese and lard. It's also the fat that you find on red meat. In general this type of fat is best avoided, as a diet too high in saturated fats can lead to obesity, heart disease and other health problems.

## Unsaturated fats

In contrast, these fats usually come from vegetable sources. Oils made from foodstuffs such as olive, sunflower and soya all contain high levels of unsaturated fat, as do other foods such as oily fish and certain types of margarine. This type of fat is generally thought of as beneficial to health if eaten in moderation.

The current government guidelines say that we should get no more than 35 per cent of our total energy intake from fat. (In America this figure is only 30 per cent.) For a woman, this means about 76g of fat per day, and for a man, this is roughly 100g. The problem is not only that adults and children are getting more like 40 per cent of their energy from fat (according to the National Diet and Nutrition Survey of 2000), but a large proportion of that fat is saturated, not unsaturated.

In the case of children, one of the big issues is that junk food and much of the food marketed directly at children is very high in saturated fat. Some frozen burgers, for example, contain meat that is 50 per cent fat; which means that a single portion has a whopping six teaspoons of fat – even if it's grilled! Other high saturated-fat culprits include most take-out meals, such as fish and chips, kebabs, fried chicken, curries and pizzas.

# How much fat is too much?

So how do you know whether a food is high in fat or not? If you look on the back on a packet it should tell you how many grams of fat per 100g it contains, but as a very general rule:

**Very high-fat foods contain:**
**20g unsaturated fat or more per 100g.**
**5g saturated fat or more per 100g.**

**Very low-fat foods contain:**
**3g unsaturated fat or less per 100g.**
**1g saturated fat or less per 100g.**

While you may struggle to only eat foods that count as **very low fat,** you can aim towards the recommended figure of getting no more than 35 per cent of your total energy from fat by avoiding the **higher fat foods**.

To help you work out how much fat you should have per day, the current recommended daily limit is 100g for men and 76g for women. While there isn't a current RDA for children, it should clearly be less than either of these figures.

## Sugar

Children are born with a preference for sweet foods and have a natural distrust of bitter flavours. The scientific explanation is that sweetness signals that a food is full of calories, while bitterness signals the possibility of poison. In moderation, sugar does little or no harm, however, excessive consumption of sugar can lead to obesity and tooth decay (see Tooth decay, opposite). Although the research has thus far proved inconclusive, many parents and teachers also believe that sugar has adverse effects on children's behaviour, encouraging hyperactivity or energy swings.

Children aged between seven and ten years old consume, on average, more than half a kilo of sugary food every day. The worst offenders are soft drinks – a standard can of cola, for example, contains a staggering nine teaspoons of sugar (35g) – and energy drinks are even worse. Other high-sugar foods include flavoured yoghurts, sugary breakfast cereals, cakes, biscuits, sweets, chocolate, puddings and ice cream.

### What is it?

Dental decay is a breakdown of the normal hard tissues on the outer surface of the teeth to form a soft cavity or hole. In severe decay, the cavity may be very deep, affecting the nerve and blood vessels.

### What causes it?

The bacteria that thrive on the teeth are responsible for decay, particularly when there's a large amount of sugary food debris left in the mouth. These bacteria grow in a sticky coating on the teeth called plaque. They break down these food sugars into acids that etch away at the surface enamel. Frequent consumption of sugary foods and drink increases the risk of decay, especially if they are allowed to surround the teeth for long periods of time (for example, if teeth aren't regularly brushed or if a baby sucks on a bottle full of sweet drink).

### How do sugars attack your teeth?

Invisible germs (bacteria) live in your mouth all the time and some of these form the sticky material called plaque on the surface of the teeth. When you

# Hot topic **Tooth decay**

put sugar in your mouth, the bacteria in the plaque gobble up the sweet stuff and turn it into acids. These acids are powerful enough to dissolve the hard enamel that covers your teeth, leaking out the calcium and phosphate minerals and softening and destroying the enamel and dentine below. That's how cavities get started. If you restrict your sugar intake, the bacteria can't produce as much of this acid.

## Who's affected?

Dental decay is very common. The addition of fluoride to toothpaste has helped to protect teeth and reduce decay, but the continual trend towards sweeter snacks in children's diets is working against these precautions.

At first, tooth decay may not cause any obvious symptoms – especially in milk teeth – but as it progresses it may cause toothache, or sensitivity to hot or cold, or very sweet foods.  If the nerve becomes affected an infection may establish and lead to an abscess, which brings with it severe pain, swelling of the jaw and fever.

## What can I do to prevent my child getting tooth decay?

* Limit your child's intake of sugary food and drinks.
* Discourage grazing – snacking on sugary treats is actually worse than eating all your sweets in one go.
* Set a good example yourself.
* Think about what you buy – check the food labels for added sugar.
* Make sure your children clean their teeth regularly – they need to brush every morning and evening and after a sugary snack.

# How much sugar is too much?

Sugar is the only food stuff that is not actually needed by the body. For this reason, there is no recommended daily intake, so instead the World Health Organisation offers figures for the maximum intake.

This quantity is no more than ten per cent of a child's total calorie intake per day coming from added sugar. Based on 4g of sugar in a teaspoon this equates to roughly:

* 11 teaspoons or 45g for children aged five to nine.
* 12 teaspoons or 50g for children aged 10-14 years old.
* 16 teaspoons or 65g for children 15 and over.

Remember that this maximum amount doesn't just include teaspoons of sugar added to drinks, but includes the sugar content of all sugary foods such as sweets, cakes and fizzy drinks. For example:

* One can of coke contains nine teaspoons or 35g of sugar.
* 100g of Kellogs Frosties contains 9 teaspoons or 38g of sugar.
* 100g of Sugar Puffs contains 12 teaspoons or 49g sugar.

## Sugar cravings

The body often yearns for sugar, but there are ways to control these sugar cravings. To do this, you need to know more about 'good' and 'bad' types of sugar: 'bad' sugars – simple sugars and highly refined grains in foods such as white flour, sweets and cakes – cause your child's blood sugar level to rise extremely quickly and then slump, with an associated mood change. Complex natural sugars, or 'good' sugars, are broken down more slowly, allowing blood sugar levels to rise more gradually. These are found in fruit and wholewheat products.

So how do you make the swap from bad to good? The key is to make sure that the majority of sugar in your child's diet is the complex natural kind, while limiting the amount of added sugar – by cutting down on soft drinks, sweets and so on. You need to start healthy habits as early as possible with your children, but the good news is that these habits will stay with them for the rest of their lives.

## Salt

Most children eat twice as much salt as the recommended daily allowance (see right). The problem is that salt is often hidden in the food that children like the most – one takeaway burger, for example, will give a young child more salt than his total daily allowance. Similarly, bread, pizzas, sausages, tinned spaghetti, soups and baked beans can often contain too much, while lunchbox favourites such as processed cheese, sliced meats and savoury snacks also tend to be high in salt. Surprisingly, even sweet products such as breakfast cereals, biscuits and hot chocolate can contain large amounts of salt.

To make matters worse, many foods have actually got saltier over the past few decades. Between the years of 1978 and 2003, for example, the average salt content in a packet of crisps has doubled.

So what's the problem? Well, according to the Food Standards Agency, eating too much salt can raise your blood pressure, thus tripling your chance of heart disease, whatever your age.

## How much salt is too much?

These are the current guidelines for salt and children per day – bear in mind that one teaspoon is the equivalent of 6g of salt. But be warned, too, that salt is also present in food as 'sodium', which is 2.5 times more concentrated than salt. In other words, if you read a label saying '1.2g sodium' then it actually contains about 3g salt.

* 1 to 3 years – 2g salt (0.8g sodium).
* 4 to 6 years – 3g salt (1.2g sodium).
* 7 to 10 years – 5g salt (2g sodium).
* 11 and over – 6g salt (2.5g sodium).

Foods that are high in salt include:
* Bacon.
* Baked beans (look for low-salt versions instead).
* Biscuits.
* Chips.
* Crisps and other salty snacks.
* Fast food, including burgers and pizzas.
* Fish in brine.
* Gravy granules.
* Ready-made cooking sauces and ready meals.
* Sausages.
* Smoked meat and fish.
* Soy sauce, stock cubes and yeast extract.
* Tinned pasta, e.g. spaghetti hoops.
* Tinned soup.
* Tinned vegetables (with added salt).

## Common barriers to healthy eating

Many parents would dearly love their children to eat a healthy diet but often find themselves running into difficulties. At the end of this chapter you'll find some general tips to help your child eat more healthily, but first let's take a look at some of the specific reasons behind why children have unhealthy diets – and, more to the point, what you can do about it.

### Fussy eaters

Food fads are surprisingly common. In fact, two thirds of children go through a stage of refusing to eat certain foods, especially between the ages of two and ten. Sometimes this is because children genuinely dislike the taste of a particular food, whereas for others fussy eating is a normal part of a child's growing sense of independence and choice. After all, adults don't like all foods, so why should we expect our children to?

Occasionally there are more complex issues behind selective eating. Young children generally have little control over their lives and so food is one of the few arenas in which they can express themselves. Refusing to eat can be a way of showing anger, anxiety or lack of attention, as well as gaining control in a relationship.

Fussy eating is almost always more distressing for the parent than for the child. When your child refuses food it can feel like a rejection of your effort and love. Children are canny observers and they can sense these feelings, which may encourage them to do it even more. But there are a lot of things you can do if your child will only eat a narrow range of foods. (See opposite.)

## Don't panic

Maintain a low-key approach when offering any food. Many experts suggest putting the food on the table and encouraging just one bite, and not reacting positively or negatively whether the child likes it or not. Above all, stay calm if your children refuse to eat something, and don't insist on a clean plate.

## No bribes

When kids are cajoled into eating a food or even rewarded or praised for eating it, the child often develops an aversion to that particular food. Try not to offer foods as rewards, or say 'there's no pudding until you've eaten all those vegetables'.

# Top tips for fussy eaters

By doing so you are simply reinforcing the idea that the pudding is more desirable than the vegetables.

## Out with the junk

Pack the refrigerator and the cupboards with healthy foods, only put balanced meals on the table and keep all other undesirable foods out of the house. It's best to keep less healthy food away from temptation, and then bring it in on special occasions when you let the children have control over eating it.

## One at a time

When it comes to new foods, only offer one at a time. Children are more likely to try a new food if they have the option of not swallowing it.

## Hide the veg

If your child has an aversion to veg, try putting them in a cheese sauce or blending them in a soup. Children also like to eat them when they are fresh and crispy, so try offering crudités – clean, crisp, fresh vegetables cut into strips to be eaten with fingers – with a

yoghurt dip, for example. You could even try giving them vegetable juices such as carrot or tomato juice.

## Eat together

Believe it or not, most children like eating with their parents, so try to eat something yourself with your children, even if you are planning a meal later. Children sometimes accept small tastes of alternatives from somebody else's plate – it's less overwhelming than the sight of a food they don't like in front of them.

## Tight budget

Some parents resist giving their children healthy food because they think it will cost more. According to the charity Child Poverty Action Group, low-income families often know what healthy food they should buy but many struggle to afford even the basics. However, the picture isn't as straightforward as it would first appear. While certain healthier foods sometimes carry a heftier price tag – for example, organic or biodynamic – many healthy foods cost the same or even less than unhealthy meals. Ready meals, processed food and take-aways are often more expensive than fresh food, comparatively, because you are paying someone to make the meal, in addition to covering their raw material costs.

So it doesn't have to cost more to eat healthily; you just need to plan a little and know where and when to buy. Here are some tips on how to have a healthy diet on a budget:

## Eating healthily without breaking the bank

* If you shop at the end of the day, you'll often find that perishable foods such as bread, meat and veg are reduced in price.

* Fruit and veg in season are cheaper and usually contain less pesticides, for example, satsumas in winter, cherry tomatoes in summer.

* Avoid bags of pre-made salad – individual lettuces will go further, last longer and cost less.

* Buy lean meat. It might be a little more expensive, but there's less waste and less fat.

* Oily fish such as mackerel, herring and sardines are cheaper than other varieties, but just as good for you.

* Frozen and tinned fruit and veg are usually cheaper and allow you to use what you need and store the rest. You might not realize, too, that frozen food also contains the same vitamin and mineral levels as fresh.

* Wholegrain and wholemeal starchy foods, such as brown rice and wholemeal bread are filling, cheap, and nutritious.

* Buy economy and own-label brands for basic items like tinned tomatoes – they're always cheaper and usually just as good.

* Plan your shopping before you go. Make a list but be flexible if a good offer turns up. Be wary of gimmicks – end-of-aisle displays are not always special offers.

* Make a few portions of meals at once and freeze them. It's the cheapest and most time-efficient way of cooking.

## School dinners and snacks

Many parents say that they try to feed their children healthy food but their attempts are ruined by the fact that school dinners are so awful, and because their children are snacking during the day when out of sight of mum and dad.

TV chef Jamie Oliver, in his recent Channel 4 series *Jamie's School Dinners*, highlighted the poor standard of many school lunches and showed that our children often sat down to a midday meal which consisted largely of chips, processed chicken nuggets, pizzas and sugar-laden puddings. The good news is that, due in large part to Jamie's 'Feed Me Better' campaign, the government has pledged an extra £280m to tackle the school meals crisis in England. Foods that are high in fat, salt or sugar are also to be banned from meals and vending machines in English schools from next September.

In the meantime, many children have returned to the good old days of taking their own packed lunches. In fact, nine out of ten children now take a packed lunch to school. So surely a meal prepared by parents will be healthier than a school dinner? Well, not necessarily.

A recent study by the Food Standards Agency found that parents were packing their children off to school with lunchboxes filled with saturated fat, sugar and salt. The study revealed that the average lunchbox contained double the recommended lunchtime intake of saturated fat and sugar, and half the total daily recommended intake of salt. Foods such as crisps, fatty spreads, cheese products, chocolate bars and biscuits were to blame for the high levels of saturated fat; white bread, crisps and processed meats explained the high salt intake; while fruit squashes, chocolate-covered bars, biscuits and yoghurts sent sugar levels sky-high. Three out of four lunchboxes failed to meet government nutritional standards for school meals, under a fifth of lunchboxes (16 per cent) did not contain starchy food such as sandwiches, pasta or rice, and half the lunchboxes (48 per cent) lacked even a single portion of fruit or veg. So what can you give to your child at lunchtime?

## Did you know?
A typical school lunchbox contains double the recommended intake of saturated fat, and sugar.

Source: Food Standards Agency

# Top tips for school lunches

✽ Keep it varied and interesting. Don't always go for sandwiches – bagels, baps, wraps and pitta breads are great alternatives.

✽ Prevent bread from being too dry by using low-fat mayo, light cream cheese or a drizzle of yoghurt instead of butter.

✽ Swap fizzy sugary drinks for real fruit juice, semi-skimmed milk, mineral water or low-sugar cordials.

✽ Children love tiny treats – mini boxes of sultanas, a flapjack, yoghurt-covered raisins or a little tub of fruit salad will go down well.

## Family meals

If a family doesn't eat together it can often be difficult to know whether your children are eating healthily or not. A recent Gallup poll found that a quarter of all children in the UK eat their evening meal off a tray sitting in front of the telly. Even more worryingly, *Mother & Baby* magazine's 'Feeding The Family Survey' in 2004 discovered that 48 per cent of all toddlers eat on their own in front of the TV, rather than at the table with the rest of the family.

This is bad news for three reasons. Firstly, because research has shown that people who eat whilst sitting in front of the television tend to have a higher calorie intake than those who sit at the table. (This is because you are too distracted to notice whether you are feeling full.) Secondly, adverts shown during children's television are often for junk food and sweets, making them more appealing to young appetites. And finally, because it's a missed opportunity – the evening meal is probably one of the best, and only, times for a family to sit down and socialize together; a time that they can eat, share experiences and communicate with other members of the family. For young children this is especially important as sitting with other people and seeing them eat a variety of foods encourages the child to also want to try a variety of foods. So, when you're at the end of a busy day, what's the best way to get everyone together and eating healthily?

### ✳ Set a good example

It's no use trying to get your kids to eat healthily if you don't yourself. Children learn their eating habits from their parents, so it's vital that you set a good example. The whole family will need to eat healthily, not just the children.

### ✳ Love good food

Healthy eating shouldn't be miserable. A solitary lettuce leaf on a plate is no-one's idea of a pleasurable meal. Encourage your kids to develop an interest in good food – take them to farmers' markets and delicatessens, try new and exciting cuisines from different cultures, teach them to care about where their food comes from and buy them cookbooks. Learning to appreciate real food and real flavours will help them to reject the artificial flavours of processed food.

### ✳ Reclaim family mealtimes

Eating together as a family is one of the most important ways to change your child's eating habits. It's also a wonderful way for the family to get to know each other again.

# Kris' Top Tips

**✳ Teach your children to cook**

Getting older children involved in the actual cooking of family meals is not only a great way of encouraging them to help out around the house, but it also teaches them a valuable life skill for the future. Younger children can help out too – there are lots of great no-cook recipes, such as fruit salads, smoothies, sandwiches and frozen yoghurt.

**✳ Don't sweat about the small stuff**

It's much more important to get your child's overall diet sorted than to focus on the odd unhealthy snack. The main tasks should be getting your children to eat five portions of fruit and veg a day, increasing their consumption of all the vital nutrients and vitamins, and cutting down on the junk.

**✳ Become a label freak**

Know what's in the food you buy and become an avid label reader. Look out for the fat, sugar and salt content on packets and tins, and keep an eye on additives and E-numbers.

**✳ Be wary of 'children's food'**

Don't assume that just because a food product is aimed at children that it'll be healthy. These foods are often low in essential nutrients but high in fat, salt and sugar, relying on artificial colourings and flavourings for their appeal. So-called 'lunchbox' foods, take-aways and children's soft drinks can be the worst culprits.

**✳ Keep an eye on TV-watching habits**

The television can have a detrimental effect on children's food habits in a number of ways. Spending too long in front of the telly can fuel a child's desire for junk food by exposing them to adverts – cartoon characters and superheroes in particular are used to help sell nutritionally-poor food to children. A child who watches lots of TV also get less exercise and, if he or she eats in front of it, has a greater risk of over-eating.

**✳ Establish habits as early as possible**

Good eating habits should begin as soon as possible. Getting your child hooked on junk food will strengthen their preference for it, while getting them used to fresh food at an early age should have the opposite effect.

**✳ Keep it in perspective**

Changing your child's diet won't happen overnight and you may have the occasional battle on your hands. The key is to keep a sense of perspective and remain calm.

## Getting the family to eat together

✳ Don't set rigid, unachievable goals. If eating together every day is almost impossible, set a target of three to four meals a week.

✳ Turn the TV off to ensure quality time for conversations.

✳ Have some guidelines, such as no fighting or teasing.

✳ Try not to control conversations and/or suppress children's opinions at the table.

✳ Plan ahead to anticipate work, school and other activities that may affect the timing of meals.

✳ If you're not used to eating together it may be difficult at first and conversation may be slow. Persevere, and it will undoubtedly get easier.

✳ If you think the children would enjoy it, get them involved in making the dinner. Depending on their age, they could help with the cooking, preparing ingredients, setting the table, and so on.

Mum Tanya, step-dad Paul and their children, 11-year-old Ryan and nine-year-old Jessica, are from Essex. The family all took full advantage of Paul's job as a vending machine distributor by indulging in the mountains of sweets and goodies he brought home from work each week. It might have been a perk of the job, but Paul's regular deliveries were taking their toll on the children; the pair had around six times the recommended amount of sugar in their diet.

By consuming this much sugar both Ryan and Jessica were at risk of Type-2 diabetes. Jessica was also eating so much unhealthy food that she became severely undernourished, while Ryan lacked the essential vitamins B and C, making him more likely to suffer from mood swings. So what did Kris recommend?

# Case Study **The Swains**

## Ban those sweets

Chocolates, sweets, fizzy drinks; they all had to go. Although the Swains weren't keen on giving up their stack of sweeties, a glimpse into the childrens' future health and wellbeing was enough to stir them into action. By substituting the sweets for fruit or low-fat snacks, the children could still eat when they were peckish but without the damage. It was also important for Tanya and Paul to remove all the tempting goodies from the house.

Changing Jessica's diet so radically had some side effects (including sugar withdrawal symptoms such as headaches, fatigue and low moods), but Kris showed how important it was for Jessica to keep eating healthily so that her body could start to stabilize.

## Fresh food

To encourage the Swains to buy fresh food rather than relying on processed meals, Kris sent the family to a farm to learn what fresh food really is and where it comes from. By sending Ryan and Jessica to milk cows, collect eggs and pick fruit, the children really started to appreciate fresh food. Tanya was also advised to give Ryan and Jessica plenty of healthy snacks in their lunchboxes to encourage them to reach for something healthy rather than the usual sweets. Part of the Swains' bad eating habits were just down to routine, so by introducing a new routine Tanya could help address the problem.

## Children in the kitchen

Getting Ryan and Jessica involved in cooking was one way to make them start thinking about what they were eating. It also helped their confidence and independence by learning one of life's essential basic skills. By getting Ryan to help make healthy fruit smoothies for breakfast, Tanya was able to get him to eat one of the five portions of fruit and vegetables he needs each day.

Getting the children interested in cooking meant they're also more likely to try new things in the future, which means that Tanya can introduce them to more varied and healthy meals.

And so far this approach seems to have worked. The family have dumped the junk food and are now happily eating nutritious foods and even spending time together as a family preparing these new healthy meals!

# 2

# Exercise

If you're tired, stressed and busy, it can seem a blessed relief if your children will play computer games or gaze at the TV for hours. Unfortunately, while it can be tempting to let them be couch-potatoes, lack of physical activity is bad news for their health, development and wellbeing – and you're missing out on a brilliant way to have fun as a family.

## Are your children getting their hour per day?

So how much exercise do your children get? Lots of parents have a vague idea of how much junk food their children eat and how long they spend in front of the TV, but have you ever stopped to work out how much exercise they get each week? If the answer is no, then it's something you need to find out now and keep an eye on.

It's fairly easy to work out approximately how much exercise a child is getting; you'll have to ask them how many activities they are involved with away from home or at school, but you can keep a note of what they do in or around the house. In a single week, try to keep a chart like the one below.

At the end of the week, make a note of the difference between how much exercise your children actually get, and how much they should be getting (one hour a day). This way you'll be able to see whether they are on target. If they're not, it's time to start making some changes.

## Let's get active!

So it's simple: children need at least one hour of exercise a day. But here's the good news – that doesn't mean that they have to do a full hour of sport every day; the following activities are just as beneficial:

**A brisk walk** – for example, to school or back, to the shops, or to see a friend.
**Energetic playground activity** – playing football, tag, hopscotch or skipping.
**Time spent playing active games** – either in the back garden or in the park (such as playing tag with brothers and sisters, or football).
**A cycle ride** – round to see a friend, or in the park.

| | Time spent (minutes) | | | | | | |
| --- | --- | --- | --- | --- | --- | --- | --- |
| | MON | TUES | WED | THURS | FRI | SAT | SUN |
| Walking to and from school | | | | | | | |
| Walking/cycling to friends' houses | | | | | | | |
| Outside activities with friends | | | | | | | |
| Playing games in the park | | | | | | | |
| Organized sport (at school) | | | | | | | |
| Energetic activity in the playground | | | | | | | |
| Family sport/exercise | | | | | | | |
| Organized sport outside school | | | | | | | |
| TOTAL | | | | | | | |

## Role models

Imagine that you're standing at the fitness section in the video shop wondering which workout video to buy for yourself. Which one would you buy – the one with the fit, slim trainer with muscles in all the right places, or the one who's overweight, sitting on a sofa, and looks like they last went for a run in 1985?

Now think about that in relation to your children and how they view exercise. You keep telling them to get out and about, but when did you last go for a run or play a game of squash? One of the most important principles to bear in mind regarding children and exercise is that they look to you for an example. If you take regular exercise then they are more likely to; if you play team sport then they are more likely to join in too.

It doesn't matter if you're just not the sporty type. Don't worry if you weren't much good at sport at school, or you have a disability of some sort – there are always ways to make sure you get exercise. Take a walk to the top of the hill and back every day, go out and do a bit of gardening regularly, or walk the dog. By getting out there you'll be doing something for yourself, but you'll also be setting a vital example to your children.

Perhaps you had some unhappy experiences whilst playing sport or exercising when you were younger? Perhaps a teacher or coach was too hard on you, or maybe you suffered some painful injuries? Or maybe you just didn't enjoy sport. Whatever your reasons, it's really important that you don't let these negative feelings get in the way of your children getting into exercise. Be enthusiastic, and you never know – you might find yourself enjoying something now that you didn't when you were younger.

Even if you already get plenty of exercise, don't just sign up your children for ballet classes and football coaching and then watch from the sidelines – get involved yourself, if you can. Even better, try to think of ways that you and your children can exercise together.

## Sporting heroes

How many children have wanted to become pop stars after seeing their favourite singer on *Top of The Pops*? Well the same is equally true of sport: children love role models and heroes.

The recent success of the England cricket team is a good example. Back in 1981, when Ian Botham beat Australia almost single-handedly, an entire nation of schoolchildren were enthralled and as a result, the numbers of children taking up cricket in the following couple of years soared. In 2005, with England winning the Ashes for the first time in 18 years, the same thing is happening again. In many places throughout England, cricket clubs are reporting a 100 per cent rise in new child members – all of them wanting to be the next Freddie Flintoff.

If your child asks you one day if they can have a poster of David Beckham, or Freddie Flintoff, by all means buy them one, but don't stop there – ask them if they'd like to join a local sports team, too. Following a hero is a brilliant way to get children enthusiastic about sport.

## Sporting events

Taking your children to see sporting events is a wonderful way to introduce them to sport and exercise. Sport on TV is fine, but it is nowhere near as exciting as going to see it live – let them soak up the atmosphere at a football or cricket match, or the excitement at a motor race, to name just a few examples. Children are far more inspired by seeing sportsmen and women performing up close than on the telly.

However, it doesn't just have to be something obvious such as taking them to see a football match. What about a major athletics event or, if they like horses, how about showjumping?

Be imaginative and try lots of events to see which ones your children enjoy the most. Whatever the sport, it'll be a brilliant outing for the family, something totally different to what you usually do and, you never know, it might really inspire your children to take up a sport.

## Use your enthusiasm

Which sports do you enjoy? Athletics, a game of cricket, or perhaps something more graceful such as ice skating? Whatever sport or activity you're thinking of getting your children involved in, showing enthusiasm for it is one of the best ways to get them interested. It's the same with food – show them that you enjoy eating healthy food and they're much more likely to enjoy it too. Of course, the sports and activities that you're most likely to show enthusiasm for are usually the ones that you enjoy yourself.

## Joint activities

If you've never done much exercise with your children, there are enormous benefits you might have never thought of. For instance:

**Safety** If you worry a lot about your child's safety, or perhaps if you live in an area where it's not safe for your children to play outside, this is an excellent way of getting your children to exercise while also being able to keep an eye on them.

**Shy children** If your children are shy, or lack confidence, exercising with them will help to gently introduce them to physical activity and the outdoors, without them feeling they're on their own.

**Bonding** Playing together helps you bond with your children. You may find you spend a huge amount of time telling them what to do and what not to do, but having fun as a family is really important and if you take time to do it, they'll feel like you understand them better.

**Sociability** If it's difficult for your children to play with others because of where they live, joining in with them might well be one of the only ways you'll be able to get them to exercise. Children who don't live close to friends often don't want to go out on their own to the park or to a sporting event – it's just no fun having no-one to play with.

## Finding sports in your area

Not sure where to start when it comes to finding sports for your children to do in the local area? It's actually much easier than you think.

### School

One of the best places to start is at your child's local school. Despite the decline in the hours each week that are dedicated to PE in most schools, after-school sports clubs are still thriving. Not only do these offer a great opportunity for your child to be involved in team sports, but you can also feel confident that the activities are supervised by a responsible adult. School sports foster friendships between children while also helping to develop a feeling of pride; both of which are hugely beneficial for any child.

Parents can get involved with their child's school sports in lots of ways. There's a reliable body of data that suggests that the more practical support and encouragement parents, siblings and friends provide, the more likely they are to get involved in, and keep up with, a sport. Depending on the level of involvement that your child feels comfortable with (and it must be their choice), you can cheer from the sidelines, coach a team, make the half-time teas or simply offer your services as a taxi to take the children to home or away games. Even if they don't want you present at the games, you can still provide support in the form of washing their sports kit, altering meal times to accommodate fixtures and taking an interest in their game.

Sometimes schools organize sports-based trips. Despite the fact that school trips have received bad press in the past few years (see Chapter 9 on Safety, for more information), school outings are still one of the safest ways for your child to be involved in sport. If at all possible, allow your child to go on these trips – whether it's a weeks skiing or a weekend outward bound course. Children almost invariably get a lot out of these trips in terms of confidence, exercise and independence.

## Sports centres and gyms

If your child fancies a sport that isn't connected to their school, why not check out what facilities or instruction is offered by the local authority? Your local sports centre is a great place to start and will often have events specially designed for children to take part in. To find out what's going on in your area, contact your local council, who is responsible for running all the public sports centres in your area. If you have access to a computer, you can search for local facilities by going onto your city council website – it's usually the name of your town or city followed by .gov.uk (for example Southampton City Council is www.southampton.gov.uk). Alternatively, you can search through the local phone book, which will list all the sports centres in your area. The great thing about local authority sports centres is that they represent good value for money and, in many cases, will only charge minimal fees for children's sports. Your child will also get the opportunity to mix with a fantastic range of children.

If you're a member of a private gym, why not ask whether they have activities for children? Young people often get discounted rates for joining, or you could think about a family membership. Private gyms often have kids' clubs, too, which offer supervised physical activities for your children to enjoy while you exercise elsewhere without worrying about keeping an eye on them.

# How to teach your child to ride a bike

* Always make sure that your child **cycles safely** and with care and attention to everything that is happening around them.
* Always ensure they wear a **helmet**, along with protective pads for knees and elbows. These pads can be removed once the child is confident of their cycling ability, but the helmet must always be worn.
* Always choose a flat area of land **away from dangers** such as broken glass, uneven gravel paths, broken posts and objects sticking out of the ground.
* Always ensure that there is a lot of **forward-facing space** for the child to get their bearings and balance.
* Put your child on the bike and hold onto one handlebar and the back of their sweatshirt (like a handle). Have the child begin to pedal while you help steer. Your child will feel the wobble of the bike, and you shouldn't try to prevent this as they will learn to balance using the wobble as a guide. Reassure the child that you are there with them and will stay right there.

* After a few lessons, let go of the handlebar (you, not the child!), and hold onto the back of their sweatshirt only. This gives them new sense of freedom, and within a short period of time you won't even have to hold on to their sweatshirt.
* This will not be a skill that they learn overnight. It is likely to be highly frustrating for both parents and children. Then, one day, off they go, riding a two-wheeled bike as if they were born on it!
* NB – Falling is a fact of life: reassure your child that falls will happen, but they are part of the learning process. Understanding this, your child will soon be a confident cyclist.

## Sports Clubs

There are lots of websites that will help you to locate a sports club in your area. Sport England is an organization committed to creating opportunities for people to start in sport, stay in sport and succeed in sport. Part of their website, called Active Places (www.activeplaces.com), allows you to search for sports facilities anywhere in England and has information on over 50,000 facilities nationwide. Whether you're looking for a swimming pool or a ski centre, it's the best place to start.

If you have a specific sport in mind, say football or swimming, most sports have a professional association which can help you locate your nearest club. Try My Sport at www.trymysport. co.uk – it has a directory with contact details for almost every sport your children could wish to try, from aikido to yachting.

If you want to get involved too, consider becoming a sports volunteer. Local clubs are always on the lookout for unpaid help – in fact, nearly 1.5 million people are sports volunteers up and down the UK. It doesn't matter if you are not particularly proficient in a sport – clubs need people with bags of enthusiasm and commitment above anything else.

## Family activities

If your children are reluctant to join a local club – maybe they feel nervous about being away from you or would prefer to do a more informal activity – there are lots of ways you can get active as a family without spending a fortune. Here are just a few ideas:

We usually think of walking and hiking as things we do in the countryside but if you live in the middle of a city, that's no reason not to travel a short distance to go for a walk, or consider organizing an urban hike and take in the sights as you go. Make use of local sports grounds and parks – children love a game of five-a-side or a knockabout. Get friends and parents involved for a full game, but if you haven't got enough people try playing penalties or kicking tries. Rounders, softball and French cricket are also perfect park games for a sunny day.

Children go absolutely mad for adventure playgrounds – so much so that it's worth travelling a good distance to find one. They're physical, but they also incorporate a variety of activities to keep children interested – as well as an element of exploration and creativity, such as thinking of imaginative ways to get from A to B. You can either join in or watch from a safe distance!

Swimming baths also offer low-cost, high-fun exercise for all the family. Children can either swim lengths or just mess about – both are brilliant workouts and will help your children become confident around water. You can also get other children to come along and make it even more sociable. Local pools also offer swimming classes if your child needs tuition.

# Hot topic **Sporty and unsporty children**

## What if your child is simply not sporty?

Time to explode a common myth. There is simply no such thing as an 'unsporty' child. Usually, if a child is persistently shying away from exercise, it's either because the conditions aren't right (for example, they're in a place or with people they don't like), or because they're simply not playing the right sport for them. There is a sport or activity to suit every child, so experiment to find the right one for your child.

The health implications of exercise are too important to let your children get away with doing nothing. You need to find ways to get your child to enjoy exercise, even if they do seem to be the indoors type.

## The non-competitive child

Many individuals might not necessarily take to the competitive side of sport, and there are as many reasons why. Encourage your child to do well, but don't push them too hard – if they're not enjoying something, they're less likely to continue doing it later in life. If you're playing a sport against your child, make sure they can experience the genuine thrill of winning. As discussed on page 48, give yourself a points handicap and give your child a bit of a chance.

## Don't feel as passionate as them about their sport of choice?

Unfortunately, it's bad luck for you. You must encourage your children in whichever sport they choose, even if it's not something that you yourself would enjoy.

## Fear that a child will not excel at a chosen sport

This thought crosses the minds of many parents when their child expresses an interest in sport – especially something with quite distinct physical associations, such as rugby, martial arts, or even ballet. It is vital that you keep any doubts about their ability to yourself. Remember that, although some challenges can seem daunting, it can give a child an amazing confidence boost to achieve something they're passionate about, despite the odds. So, have confidence in them and believe they can do well, whatever your immediate feelings are. Don't underestimate them, or their determination to succeed. Let them find out for themselves whether or not an activity is right for them.

## Let your child choose

All children are different. It's obvious really, but it's amazing how much difference there can be (even between young children of the same sex) in terms of what they enjoy and what they don't. Some children revel in the outdoors, some couldn't think of anything worse; some children love being taught a new game or skill, and some just like being left to their own devices.

If your children are at the age when parents are just too embarrassing for words and they'd rather be seen dead than be seen exercising with mum and dad, then there are lots of sports they can try by themselves. Your children will love the sense of independence it gives them and you can relax in the knowledge that they're getting fit and healthy in the process.

The table below is designed to help you think about what your child might enjoy. Think about each of these preferences and how your child fits into them. Are they mad keen on water? Do they like inventing their own games? Don't forget there are loads of other activities that are not mentioned here; it's not a complete list. For example, there's a wide range of team sports they can try other than football, rugby, cricket and netball.

## Children's exercise preferences

| | | | |
|---|---|---|---|
| Likes team sports | Football, rugby, cricket, netball | Prefers individual sports | Tennis, squash, athletics, watersports |
| Likes sociable sports | Team sports, athletics | Prefers solitary sports | Jogging, cycling, swimming |
| Likes competing | Tennis, football, athletics | Plays more to enjoy it | Climbing, hiking, skiing, horse riding |
| Likes the outdoors | Hiking, skiing, cycling | Prefers the indoors | Swimming, ballet, squash |
| Likes being coached | Swimming, gymnastics, horse riding, athletics, dance | Prefers teaching themselves | Skateboarding |
| Likes a pure physical challenge | Gym sessions, running, aerobics | Enjoys a mental challenge too | Orienteering, dance classes |
| Likes family activities | Hiking, skiing, cycling, swimming | Prefers time away from the family | Skateboarding, ballet, gymnastics |
| Likes combative sports | Rugby, fencing, martial arts | Likes gentle sports | Ballet, dance, gymnastics, ice skating, horse riding, yoga |
| Likes doing what other children do | Football, skate boarding, horse riding | Likes doing something different to other children | Martial arts, gymnastics |

Knowing your child really helps here, but if you're not sure, don't worry. Instead, encourage them to try lots of different things, and see what they enjoy best. Every dad wants their son to play football for their country, but wouldn't we be just as proud if it turned out to be cycling or squash?

Try not to assume too much about what your child will like because of their sex, age or physical shape. We tend to assume that boys like football and girls like ballet – but that's not always true. If your daughter suddenly announces that she wants to give karate a go, why not? Correspondingly, if your son is quite small for his age, rugby might not seem like the ideal sport – but you never know.

## Children – dedicated followers of fashion

Almost all children like the feeling of being cool and fashionable and therefore popular with their peers. This may be more important for some than others, but it's a pretty universal theme these days. Peer pressure will affect your children in all sorts of ways during their childhood (and later on, for that matter), and sometimes in unhealthy ways.

The good news is that, unlike other forms of peer pressure, when it comes to exercise, peer pressure is not entirely a bad thing. At the end of the day, you want your children to enjoy sport and exercise. So, if your child wants to do a certain activity because their friends are doing it, why not? Let them give it a try – encourage them as you would for any other interest.

Children are no different when it comes to sports and activities. From a very early age, they learn that certain sports and activities have a 'cool' factor that others don't. Here are just a few common 'cool' examples:

* Skateboarding.
* Snowboarding.
* Roller-blading.
* Ice hockey.
* Martial arts (e.g. Karate, Tae-kwon-do).
* Horse riding.
* Ballet.

The last two on this list might not seem that cool, but they illustrate the point that the 'cool' factor can be an incentive for children to get involved in almost anything. If other children at school are doing it, they'll want to as well. Peer pressure doesn't work only for the latest 'in thing' though – it can make a child want to play a really popular sport, such as football.

One problem that can crop up is cost. Very few parents can afford to indulge every whim of their child. Most children at some stage have demanded something for Christmas, such as a pair of roller blades or a skateboard, which has then not been used after Boxing Day. If your child wants to try something new, be totally supportive – but if it involves significant cost up front, make it clear that they have to give it a proper go, and not just give up if they're bored after the first session. A sensible way to limit costs is to start off with second-hand equipment and then buy brand new gear if they keep up the interest. Internet auction sites are great for finding second-hand sports equipment.

## Be a role model

It's no use telling your children they should do more exercise if they see you slobbing in front of the TV every night. Your children will follow your example, so dust off those trainers and get active!

## Be supportive

For children to participate in their chosen sport they sometimes need a lot of input from their parents. This can translate as lifts to and from the sports venue, your presence as a spectator to cheer them along, or just flexibility in moving around mealtimes to accommodate games and practice sessions.

## Have faith

You need to believe that your child can be good at sport – children are quick to pick up on any doubts you may have about their physical abilities. Let them work out for themselves what they can and can't do.

## Love the outdoors

While rainy days can sometimes prevent you from playing sport, nothing should stop you from taking exercise outdoors.

# Kris' Top Tips

Children need fresh air and they also need to expand their horizons and be confident away from home. Wrap up warm and go splash in the puddles!

## Limit the TV

While television has its uses on occasion, too much telly can prevent your child from getting physical exercise. It also encourages bad eating habits and weight gain. (See Chapter 1.)

## Walk or cycle to school

If it's safe to do so, encourage your children to walk or cycle to school. If you are worried about your child travelling alone, why not encourage them to walk or cycle with a friend, or accompany them yourself?

## Start them young

The younger you get your children into exercise and sport, the better. An active child is much more likely to be an active adult.

## Play and have fun

Physical exercise doesn't have to mean competitive sport – children also need to be allowed to simply play. A knockabout in the park is just as beneficial as playing sport in a top league. Encourage them simply to have fun and enjoy themselves.

## Get involved

Local clubs always need volunteers to help them coach or manage a team, so why not get involved? If you don't want to be a coach you could always help in other ways – by cheering loudly or making the half-time refreshments. This will allow you to enjoy an activity with your child and show them that you support what they're doing.

## Don't push

Above all, children need to choose their own physical exercise or sport. As a parent the best thing you can do is to find out what your child is interested in and then offer gentle encouragement.

The Reynolds skipped seaside activities in their home town of Blackpool in favour of more sedate pastimes, such as watching TV, munching on snacks and playing darts. When the parents, Alma and Ian, spent time with their only son Michael (aged seven), it usually ended up being a couch-marathon in front of the TV. To make matters worse, Michael's diet was anything but healthy, with a standard breakfast consisting of two waffles with syrup, two rashers of bacon, two sausages, a fried egg, beans, hash browns and toast. He also had an aversion to fruit, vegetables or anything remotely healthy, instead guzzling his way through dozens of salty snacks and sweet treats a week.

This poor diet, combined with a chronic lack of exercise, was starting to take its toll on Michael and his confidence was suffering. Not only that, but Michael's chances of suffering from cancer, heart disease or a stroke were dramatically higher than his peers, so much so that Michael was given a dismal life expectancy of just 59. So, what did Kris recommend?

# Case Study **The Reynolds**

### Take up judo

Kris enrolled Michael in a judo class as a way of encouraging him into a more structured exercise programme. The aim was to get Michael to regularly participate in two hours of activity a week. Becoming involved in a new sport would help develop Michael's social skills by making him interact with children of his age. It would also help his fitness, and in turn improve his self-confidence.

### Get mum involved

Because Michael relied heavily on his mother's support, Alma was encouraged to take Michael to his first lesson and sit on the sidelines to watch him. Judo is a sport that is beneficial for youngsters for more than just health reasons. The way the training is divided into levels means that it sets clear goals for children to work towards and to achieve on a regular basis. The completion of such goals works as a positive boost for any child, and with correct training and sustained interest from the individual, these are always attainable.

### On yer bike

Although he was seven years old, Michael had never learned to ride a bike. So Kris set this as his goal for developing a new skill. The idea was to develop confidence and a feeling of independence. By mastering something new, Kris hoped that Michael would feel less reliant on his parents and more in control of his life.

### Be encouraging

It was vital that Alma and Ian continued to encourage Michael, even if he found something difficult to begin with. Being encouraging without being pushy goes a long way to giving a child enough confidence to persevere and to eventually achieve their goals. By empathizing with Michael's failure, as well as sharing in his successes, Alma and Ian could show him that sticking with something, even when it gets tough, is a positive and rewarding thing to do.

Since the series Michael has has really turned his life around – not only does he still do judo and ride his bike regularly but he has also taken up the trumpet! But it's not just his confidence that has benefited from the experience, his body has too and he's already lost a stone in weight.

# 3

# Sleep

Many children get less sleep than they need. In fact, in a recent study, children were asked about their sleep patterns and as many as half said they weren't getting enough and that they found it difficult to stay awake during the day. With all the other parental worries, does it really matter if your child isn't getting a good night's rest?

## Why is sleep important?

**The best way to understand why sleep is important for children is to understand what happens when they don't get enough of it. While the occasional poor night's rest won't do any long term damage, sleep deprivation over time can have devastating consequences on schoolwork, behaviour and family life.**

**After a bad night's sleep you'll notice that the first thing to go is your ability to think clearly. Luckily, all you need is a good night's rest and you feel normal again. With chronic sleep loss, however, failing to get adequate rest night after night has a serious impact on your brain's ability to function properly. You feel groggy and forgetful, you find it more difficult to concentrate or make decisions, your attention span shortens. In fact, research has shown that after just one night's missed sleep your brain feels as fuzzy as if you had drunk two glasses of wine. Imagine how confusing and disorientating that must be for a child. It's particularly difficult for them to monitor themselves and realize they are tired if that is how they always feel.**

## Sleep and schoolwork

If sleep deprivation impairs your attention, decision-making, communication and planning abilities, it's easy to see how children with sleep problems would find life at school difficult. Sleep-deprived children perform worse on most mental tasks – about a fifth of primary school children who have sleep problems also experience academic problems. Similarly, teenagers who don't get enough shut-eye are more likely to struggle or fail at school, all things being equal.

Lack of sleep even affects the higher mental faculties, such as abstract thinking and creativity. One recent study found that a good night's sleep helped volunteers crack a complicated number puzzle they couldn't solve the day before. It's as if 'sleeping on a problem' gives your brain a chance to restructure the information and come up with a new solution.

Sleep also helps our brains to store and organize information. The brain 'rescues' memories during the night that have been lost during the previous day. In other words, things you thought you had forgotten at the end of a long day are refreshed while you sleep. Sleep also helps some memories mature while discarding other, unimportant ones.

Conversely, a bit of extra sleep seems to improve a school child's performance. A study among Israeli primary school children found that as little as one hour extra of sleep had a marked effect on their grades. The children (aged between nine and 11) were tested before and after they had either an hour's extra sleep or an hour less. The children who had the extra hour performed significantly better on memory and attention span tests compared to those who lost an hour's sleep. In fact, some of the children performed as well as children two years their senior. Reaction times were also better among the children who got an extra 60 minutes in bed.

## Sleep and behaviour

As well as school performance, lack of sleep can also have a profound impact on a child's behaviour at home. Research has shown that young children who experience sleep problems are more likely to smoke, drink or use drugs as adults. Boys are also more susceptible than girls – those who have early childhood sleep problems are more than twice as likely to have started using alcohol by age 14, to smoke, and to use illicit drugs, compared to boys who don't have sleep problems. The reasons behind this are still unclear, but one theory is that children who have never learned to sleep properly are more likely to turn to alcohol and other drugs

**Did you know?**

The world record for longest period of time a human being has gone without sleep is 264 hours, set by Randy Gardner in 1965. After 11 days awake the 17-year-old high-school student reported symptoms including slurred speech, mood swings, irritability, memory lapses, difficulty concentrating, paranoia and hallucinations.

as adults to help them to relax and unwind.

Poor sleep patterns can leave children feeling tired and irritable, making it difficult for them to socialize with friends and family. It can also result in them feeling anxious and depressed. Children with persistent sleep problems tend to have poorer relationships with their parents and other children, whereas those who sleep well usually have higher self-esteem and are better able to control their aggression.

Children who are sleepy during the daytime are more likely to be clumsy and hurt themselves in an accident. An Italian study found that young boys who slept for less than ten hours a night had a greater chance of ending up in Accident and Emergency, and that this association was particularly strong among boys attending nursery school. Both boys and girls who go to bed late are also more likely to be involved in accidents in the home, the peak time for injury being between 4pm and midnight.

Any parent will tell you that a child who hasn't slept properly is more likely to be moody and find it difficult to control their impulses and anger. They also struggle to focus on one task and are more likely to be fidgety, inattentive and disruptive. There is increasing evidence that this type of behaviour is sometimes misdiagnosed by both parents and health professionals as Attention Deficit/Hyperactivity Disorder, when the real problem is simply lack of adequate sleep.

**Did you know?**

Sleep deprivation has been blamed for some of the world's major disasters, including the Exxon Valdez oil spill, the nuclear accidents at Chernobyl and Three Mile Island, and the destruction of the space shuttle Challenger.

## Sleep and health

Sleep deprivation doesn't just have a negative impact on learning and behaviour, it can also affect your child's physical health. Disorders such as sleep apnoea (see Sleep disorders, page 66) can have a marked effect on health, leading to problems such as raised blood pressure, increased stress levels, morning headaches, failure to thrive or grow, and frequent upper respiratory infections.

Poor sleep patterns may also be linked to obesity. Hormones that control appetite and weight gain are released during sleep and research has found that people who sleep on average only five hours a night have more of the hormones which make you feel hungry and less of those which make you feel full, compared to people who sleep for eight hours. The study concludes that this difference in hormone levels increases appetite and could lead to overeating.

If poor sleep is more likely to make you obese, the bad news is that obese children are more likely to suffer from sleep problems. The link between sleep apnoea and obesity has been well documented. It's thought that 80 per cent of children who are classed as very obese also suffer from sleep apnoea. If their sleep is disrupted, an obese child is more likely to wake up feeling hungry. It's a vicious circle.

So, we know there's a problem if children persistently fail to get a good night's rest, but how much sleep is enough? Just like grown-ups, children differ considerably in their individual requirements for sleep. Some need more than others, so the best indicator is how your child feels during the day.

Over-tired children often behave in one of two ways. Sleep deprivation can leave a child feeling sluggish, tired and irritable and they may complain of feeling sleepy during the day or struggle to stay awake. Lack of sleep can also, ironically, cause over-activity or hyperactivity in a child. This is often why sleep deprivation goes unnoticed, because it appears that the child has lots of energy.

Behaviour such as impulsiveness, lack of concentration, irritability or disruptiveness can be a sign that there's a sleep problem. A child who is getting enough sleep, conversely, will be bright, alert and wide awake during the day,

# Hot topic **How much sleep do children need?**

| Age | Night-time sleep (hours) | Daytime sleep (hours) | Total sleep (hours) |
|---|---|---|---|
| 1 month | 8.5 (many naps) | 7.5 (many naps) | 16 |
| 3 months | 6–10 | 5–9 | 15 |
| 6 months | 10–12 | 3–4.5 | 14.5 |
| 9 months | 11 | 3 (2 naps) | 14 |
| 12 months | 11 | 2.5 (2 naps) | 13.5 |
| 18 months | 11 | 2.5 (1–2 naps) | 13.5 |
| 2 years | 11 | 2 (1 nap) | 13 |
| 3 years | 10.5 | 1.5 (1 nap) | 12 |
| 4 years | 11.5 | 0 | 11.5 |
| 5 years | 11 | 0 | 11 |
| 6 years | 10.5–11 | 0 | 10.5–11 |
| 7 years | 10.5 | 0 | 10.5 |
| 8 years | 10–10.5 | 0 | 10–10.5 |
| 9 years | 10 | 0 | 10 |
| 10 years | 9.5–10 | 0 | 9.5–10 |
| 11 years | 9.5 | 0 | 9.5 |
| 12–3 years | 9–9.5 | 0 | 9–9.5 |
| 14 years | 9 | 0 | 9 |
| 15 years | 8.5–9 | 0 | 8.5–9 |
| 16 years | 8.5 | 0 | 8.5 |

every day. This table shows the average recommended hours of sleep that a child needs per day, taking into account daytime naps. Note that from the age of four, which is also when they start school, children need to get all these requirements from the night-time sleep.

## What's stopping my child from getting a good night's sleep?

A child might not sleep for a number of reasons. Some problems are medical, such as sleep apnoea or restless leg syndrome, while some are behavioural, such as stress or anxiety. One of the biggest barriers to good sleep, however, is lifestyle.

### Lifestyle

A fifth of all young children get between two and five hours less sleep than they need, every night. One of the main reasons seems to be that children stay up late to play computer games or watch TV in their bedrooms and so become overstimulated by technology. They then find it difficult to unwind and get to sleep, instead of having a relaxing, calming, bedtime routine. Mobile phones are also to blame, with children regularly spending the evening texting under the bed covers when they should be asleep. When you think that over half the children in Britain have a TV in their bedroom, it's not surprising that they are finding it difficult to switch off – in both senses of the word.

Even if your child doesn't have a bedroom packed with technology, the television can still be a barrier to good sleep. Younger children who watch a lot of TV are more likely to display

bedtime resistance, take longer to fall asleep and, on average, get less sleep than those who watch less TV. The reasons for this are not entirely clear, but the fact that children who watch lots of television tend to eat badly, weigh more, take less exercise and find it difficult to have 'quiet time' must be significant.

### Bedtime routine

Lots of young children refuse to go to bed or stay in their bedroom when it's time for sleep, while other children will go to bed, but only after a great deal of fuss. This is known as 'bedtime resistance' and is one of the most common and frustrating problems that parents face. As a result, many parents simply give up and let their children dictate their own bedtime or fall asleep in front of the TV. While this is an understandable, low-hassle approach for mum and dad, the reality is that having an inconsistent or lack of bedtime routine actually makes the problem worse. Children who choose their own bedtimes rarely go up at the right time, which means they end up going to bed too late, don't get enough sleep, and feel pooped during the day.

### Diet

Diet can also play a large part in either keeping children awake or helping them to relax. Caffeine, for example, interferes

> **Did you know?**
> A fifth of all young children get between two and five hours less sleep than they need, every night.

## How much caffeine are children drinking?

| Drink | Caffeine content |
|---|---|
| Filter coffee | 200 mg |
| Instant coffee | 140 mg |
| Red Bull | 109 mg |
| Tea | 100 mg |
| Iced Tea | 70 mg |
| Diet Coke | 45 mg |
| Dr Pepper | 41 mg |
| Pepsi | 38 mg |
| Coca-Cola | 34 mg |
| Hot chocolate/cocoa | 10 mg |
| Chocolate milk | 8 mg |

Caffeine content per 12 fl oz (equivalent of a normal can or large mug).

with a child's ability to sleep. It is a stimulant – it keeps us lively and active during the day but it can also stop you from getting a good night's rest. The more caffeine a child has in their bloodstream at bedtime, the longer it will take them to fall asleep and the more disrupted their sleep will be.

We don't imagine that children drink products containing caffeine – after all, how many young children regularly drink tea or coffee? In reality, however, caffeine is present in lots of children's foods such as cola, chocolate, iced tea, coffee ice cream, as well as infant pain relievers and other over-the-counter medicines. Caffeinated energy drinks contain even more – a can of Red Bull, for example, contains 2½ times the amount of caffeine as a can of cola. Children have smaller bodies than adults, so even a tiny amount of caffeine will have a bigger effect on them and does them no good. For an idea of the caffeine content of various drinks, see the table opposite

Children who consume large amounts of fizzy drinks containing caffeine tend to take longer to get to sleep, are more likely to have broken sleep, and get less sleep overall. They also tend to be sleepier during the day than children who consume less. The problem is that caffeine drinkers often drink more caffeine during the day to compensate for the fact they feel tired, but this lethargy is because caffeine is keeping them awake at night, and so the cycle continues.

Sugar is also responsible for disrupting sleep patterns in children. Consuming lots of sugary foods or fizzy drinks, especially in the evening, can cause wakefulness and irritability due to the fact that your blood sugar levels crash in the middle of the night. The combination of caffeine and sugar found in many children's drinks, therefore, is a sure-fire recipe for a sleepless night.

## Healthy bedtime snacks

* One piece of wholemeal bread with a thin layer of smooth peanut butter.
* One banana.
* A handful of raisins.
* A small cup of sunflower seeds.
* A small bowl of plain porridge.
* One piece of wholemeal bread with a thin layer of yeast extract.
* One orange or clementine.
* A handful of blueberries or raspberries.
* Glass of skimmed milk – warm or cold.
* Warm milk with a spoonful of honey stirred in.
* Camomile, ginger, mint, lemon, peppermint or raspberry herbal tea.

### Cigarettes

Smoking is bad for young people in numerous ways but one lesser-known side-effect is its ability to interfere with sleep. Children who smoke cigarettes are more likely to have problems getting to sleep, staying asleep and will have a poorer quality of sleep. This is because nicotine is a powerful stimulant, just like caffeine, and can lead to frequent and long-lasting sleep problems. You might think that smoking doesn't affect younger children, but research shows that as many as one in ten 11–15-year-olds is a regular smoker and that every day in Great Britain about 450 children start smoking.

Passive smoking also affects a child's ability to sleep. Inhaling second-hand cigarette smoke on a regular basis can lead to respiratory illnesses, such as asthma, which are a common cause of sleep problems.

## Sleep disorders

Even if your children have a great bedtime routine, eat well and don't keep themselves awake with stimulants, they may still suffer from sleep deprivation as a result of a medical condition. At present 25 per cent of the UK population suffer from this type of sleep disorder.

### Snoring

We don't snore when we are awake because the muscles in our mouth, nose and upper throat can keep the airway open. However, when we sleep, these muscles relax. If these muscles go really floppy they partially block the airway and vibrate when we breathe in and out – this is snoring. If we have a cold or a blocked nose, the sound of these vibrations is amplified even more. Snoring is often seen as an old man's condition, but it's surprisingly common in children. There are a number of reasons why a child can snore:

∗ Obesity – this is because being overweight can lead to an increase in fat around the throat and reduced muscle tone. The airways may also be narrowed and more likely to vibrate.

∗ A child has infected tonsils or adenoids.

∗ Smoking cigarettes – smoke irritates and blocks the nasal area, making it difficult to breathe at night. Even children who passively smoke have a greater risk of snoring; children with parents who smoke are more likely to snore than children of non-smoking parents.

∗ Nasal irritation causes children with dust and pet allergies to snore. Asthmatics also tend to snore.

∗ Occasionally a child's jaw shape can cause them to snore, but this problem usually resolves itself as the child grows.

Now, we all know that snoring is annoying if you have to listen to it, but is it such a big deal if your child snores? Are they even affected by their own snoring? Well, research has shown that snoring does more than just get on the rest of the family's nerves. In a study of over 1000 children it was revealed that those who snored (which was about ten per cent) were more likely to get bad marks at school, especially in Maths and English. This is because snorers breathe in less oxygen while they're asleep, which prevents them from getting a good night's sleep and has the knock-on effect of making it more difficult for them to concentrate at school the next day.

Children whose parents snore can also be adversely affected. If an adult member of the family has a particularly loud or persistent snoring problem it can prevent the rest of the house from getting a good night's sleep.

## Sleep apnoea

An extreme version of snoring is called 'sleep apnoea'. The word apnoea comes from the Greek *apnea* which means 'want of breath' – this is because the sufferer stops breathing in their sleep and wakes up gasping for breath.

Sleep apnoea is caused by the same muscles that affect snoring – it happens when the muscles at the back of the throat and the soft palate relax to the point of blocking the airway. When this happens the sufferer can stop breathing for up to 25 seconds; the brain, which is starved of oxygen, sends an emergency signal and makes the sufferer gasp or snort for air. In a single night, a person with sleep apnoea can be woken in this way up to 350 times, which inevitably leads to tiredness the next day. Sleep apnoea has also been linked to an increased risk of strokes, heart attacks and high blood pressure.

Obese children are the most likely youngsters to suffer from sleep apnoea, but for much of the time it goes undiagnosed. In a recent study of obese children, over 85 per cent were suffering from some form of sleep apnoea, with a quarter of these suffering the most severe form of the condition. Left untreated, children with sleep apnoea may suffer daytime sleepiness resulting in poor concentration and leading to poor performance at school.

## Insomnia

Insomnia is a trickier condition to pin down. The term is used to describe a number of sleep problems including a prolonged inability to get a good night's sleep, trouble falling asleep, or waking up on a regular basis feeling unrefreshed and tired. About a third of the UK population, including children, suffers from insomnia and its effects include daytime tiredness, irritability and low moods.

It's difficult to establish the exact cause of insomnia in children, but stress and anxiety are thought to be major factors. Children who have had a recent traumatic life event, such as losing a parent or going through a family break-up, often suffer. Worries about exams, relationships and health can also severely interrupt sleep patterns. Caffeine, nicotine and high sugar foods can also exacerbate the problem.

### Restless Leg Syndrome (RLS)

The fourth of the most common medical reason behind why people fail to sleep is called restless leg syndrome. About one in 20 people suffer from this condition which causes a tingling, itching sensation or aches and pains in the legs. The sufferer has a poor night's rest because they have to keep moving their lower limbs around to relieve the discomfort.

While RLS is more common among older people, the condition can also affect children. Doctors often misdiagnose RLS in infants, mistaking it for growing pains or attention deficit disorder. Children with parents who have RLS are more likely to develop the condition than those without.

## Solving sleep problems

If your child is suffering from a sleep problem, it can be difficult to establish whether the problem lies in their diet and lifestyle or whether the condition has a medical basis. While your GP should always be your first port of call if you are worried, it might be worth thinking about whether anything at home could be causing or contributing to the problem. Often a change in bedtime routine or a reduction in certain foods can be really beneficial. Most importantly, when you decide on a bedtime routine – stick to it! There lies the success of 'routines'. If you're not sure what time your child should be hitting the hay, follow this handy guide below to help you set bed times appropriate for the age of your child.

# It's bedtime!

| Age | Suggested bedtime (based on 7am wake up) |
|---|---|
| Younger than 4 years | 7.30pm (supplemented with naps during the day – see table on page 61 for recommended amounts of sleep needed) |
| 4 years | 7.30pm |
| 5–6 years | 8pm |
| 7–8 years | 8–8.30pm |
| 9–10 years | 9–9.30pm |
| 11–14 years* | 9.30–10 pm |
| 14–16 years* | No later than 10.30pm |

*With older children it's often better not to be too rigid about bedtime: negotiate an approximate bedtime (e.g. between 9.30 and 10pm) to leave the child with some room for personal choice and manoeuvre. This will reduce the amount of bedtime conflict but once you have made the agreement you need to try and stick to it.

# Kris' Top Tips

## Make bedtime the same time every night

Believe or not, children love routines. Children have very little control over their lives, so predictability and consistency in the day can make them feel safe and secure. One of the best ways to ensure your child gets enough sleep is to set a firm and consistent bedtime. Routinely letting your child stay up late won't do them any favours, although it won't do any harm as the occasional treat, especially at weekends or school holidays.

## Create an enjoyable bedtime routine

Create a lovely, relaxing 30-minute bedtime routine for your child. It will help them wind-down and ease the transition between the noise and excitement of downstairs and the quiet darkness of the bedroom. It could include:

* A glass of warm milk *before* brushing their teeth.
* A healthy bedtime snack (see page 64).
* A relaxing bath.
* A bedtime story or lullaby.
* A gentle conversation about the day.

Keep it exactly the same every evening, so the child looks forward to the predictability of the routine.

## Take the TV out of the bedroom

Remove the TV, DVD and computer from your child's room – bedrooms are for sleeping. Older children may find this very difficult, so you might have to negotiate rules about using them instead – for instance, no playing computer games after a certain time.

## Make sure the bedroom is comfortable

Children will sleep best in a cool, dark, quiet room. The ideal temperature is 60 to 65˚F or 16 to 18˚C. You also need to make sure that noise from the rest of the house isn't disturbing them and that the room has adequate curtains or blinds – streetlights and sunrise can prevent a child from sleeping or can wake them up too early.

## Invest in a good bed

Children often get the short straw when it comes to mattresses and beds, as they tend to get hand-me-downs from older members of the family or have the cheapest bed. Don't scrimp – a good-quality mattress is vital for sleep, so invest in the best you can afford for your child and make sure, too, that you use comfortable bedding such as pure cotton sheets (artificial fibres tend to make the sheets too hot).

## Watch what and when they eat

A good diet and a healthy weight is key to good sleep. (Use Chapter 1 for advice on a balanced diet for your family.) Don't let your children eat too late – eating a large heavy meal late at night, especially if it's spicy or fatty, will interfere with their sleep. Watch the caffeine and refined sugar intake too – absolutely no caffeine or fizzy drinks after 4pm.

## Tire them out

One of the best ways to ensure that children get a good night's sleep is to encourage them to get enough physical activity during the day. (Chapter 2 gives you some great ideas for exercising the children.) Just be careful not to exercise too close to bedtime as it produces stimulants that may keep you awake for a while.

## Talk to your child

It might sound obvious, but try asking your child if there is anything that is bothering them

– worries about exams, bullying, school, family life or friendships can cause children a lot of anxiety and lead to insomnia. (Chapter 10 will help you to communicate with your child in a loving and stress-free way.)

## Look into alternative remedies

Aromatherapy can be very relaxing. The essential oils used in aromatherapy act on the nervous system and, depending on the oil you choose, can have a calming effect. Not all essential oils are suitable for children, however, but both lavender and chamomile are safe to use. Essential oils are very strong so it's vital that you follow the manufacturers instructions and never use them undiluted on the skin.

## See your GP

If you've tried everything and the problem still continues, it's a good idea to go and chat to your GP. There could be an underlying sleep disorder or sleep-disrupting allergy that needs identifying. The good news is that most sleep disorders in children can be sorted out.

LAVENDER
LAVANDULA ANGUSTIFOLIA
ESSENTIAL OIL
IS A HIGHLY CONCENTRATED PURE PLANT
DILUTE BEFORE USE eg. ADD 5

The Hammonds from Stoke-on-Trent consist of mum Michelle, dad Quentin and their boys; ten-year-old Bradley and five-year-old Joseph. When it comes to sleep Michelle and Quentin were experts in 'hands-off parenting', preferring to let Bradley and Joe do as they please and choose their bedtimes.

Unfortunately, this lack of routine and discipline at bedtime was leaving Bradley and Joe severely sleep deprived. The boys were used to parenting themselves in this area so they went to bed, and then got back up, whenever they wanted. Lack of sleep was affecting the boys'

# Case Study **The Hammonds**

concentration, memory and their performance in school. They were also more likely to pick up illnesses due to a weakened immune system. So what was the solution?

## Get into a routine

Kris set a new bedtime regime for the Hammonds, which Michelle and Quentin admitted was going to be tough to enforce. Five-year-old Joe was given a bedtime of 8pm while Bradley, who's ten, was allowed to stay up until no later than 9.30pm. This way the boys weren't staying up too late and waking up tired for school the next day. To get the boys used to their new bedtime, Michelle was given a routine of earlier dinner and bath times, which had to remain the same each day.

## Healthy bedtime snacks

To help things along, Kris recommended that the children stop eating sugary snacks and caffeine-laden drinks before bed – that meant no chocolate,

no tea, no coffee and no fizzy drinks in the evening. The high levels of sugar and caffeine in these foods were interfering with the boys' ability to get to sleep and stay asleep. Instead, if the boys wanted a snack after teatime it had to be a healthy one, such as fruit. Fizzy drinks were replaced with warm milk,

which not only quenches thirst but leaves the body feeling sleepy. And now, thanks to the new routine and healthier diet, the boys are finally benefiting from the recommended number of hours sleep per night, and this in turn has brought about real change and harmony within the whole family.

# Learning

Children are constantly learning and there is so much more to it than simply what happens at school. A child's attitude to learning is strongly influenced by that of their parents. Research shows that the amount of involvement parents have in their child's learning and education will affect their academic performance – so encourage them to enjoy it.

## Do we need a good education?

**Although it's not the only thing that brings us happiness and success, a good education gives us a real advantage in life, in more ways than one. It's amazing the number of people who say that they wish they had worked harder at school. As children, we simply don't realize what an important part education will play in the rest of our lives. By the time we're adults, we understand this link.**

## How we view learning

The general attitude to education has changed massively in Britain in the last 40 years, at every level and age group. Here's a quick example – in 1960 just one in 20 children went to university, today, that figure is one in three.

The national curriculum has changed a huge amount, too. One of the biggest changes is the greater focus on the basics, such as reading, writing and mathematics. In itself this is certainly a good thing, because it has ensured that higher numbers of children are leaving school armed with the skills that they need in order to progress in the workplace and life in general.

But these developments have also come at a cost; focusing on basic skills has meant a reduction in the number of subjects that children study at primary and secondary schools. This in turn places a greater burden on parents to provide additional teaching and to encourage a wider range of interests to help shape their children into 'rounded' adults.

## How children learn

When children start school it can be quite a relief for many parents, who suddenly find themselves with more time on their hands. Unfortunately, it's also quite tempting to think that the school will simply take over your child's education and that you can just deal with the home stuff. But if you really want to help the progress of your child's learning, you need to spend time with them before they are old enough to go to school as well as once they've started.

The first thing to do is understand the principles of learning – which effectively means knowing how young minds work – and then to learn how to help your children to keep exercising those principles.

## Concentration and attention span

Before we start, let's define these terms: concentration is the ability to focus on a single activity, or event, at the exclusion of everything else; whereas attention span is the length of time that we can maintain a basic level of concentration. These are both important skills for a child to learn.

So why is it that there is so much variation in how well children can concentrate, and how good their attention span is? The answer to this question lies in the human brain. Technically, it is an organ, but in many ways it is easier to think of it as a muscle. For basic health it needs regular exercise, just as our other muscles do, and by training the brain carefully, you can increase its abilities in many areas – memory, concentration, attention span, flexibility and imagination, to name just a few. As with physical exercise, we never know what our brains are really capable of unless they are carefully and safely stretched. And, just as in our bodies, many mental abilities can deteriorate or be lost completely if we neglect our brains.

Admittedly, there is a degree of genetic variation in terms of what we are physically capable of, and this is also true of our mental abilities. But whatever children are born with, it's what they do with their abilities that really counts – such as how well they keep their brains healthy, the extent to which they exercise them, and how much they try to explore and stretch them to their full potential.

## A lifelong love of learning

In general children, and many adults too, tend to view education and learning as a chore. It is crucial that parents avoid this attitude: very few children enjoy all of their lessons at school, but there's no reason why they shouldn't enjoy most of them. And this is where you come in.

Encourage your children to enjoy learning from the very first opportunity. This pleasure comes from the earliest days, and even in infancy we are teaching our children constantly – about food, about their environment, about discipline and about play. The sooner you steer them towards enjoying learning, the better.

∗ Encourage and guide learning at home. Make sure that your child does at least one thing a week that involves mastering something they don't study at school – it could be a musical instrument, a puzzle, or just a interest in something like cars or animals.

∗ Reward effort in both schoolwork and learning at home.

∗ Be enthusiastic about all of your children's learning.

∗ Explain to your children at every stage why something is worth learning. As adults we tend to be happier working at something when we know there is a reason for doing so, and children are usually the same.

## Parents as role models

We've seen in previous chapters how children often take their lead from their parents in all sorts of things – such as diet, exercise and sleep – but the same is also true of learning.

There are lots of ways in which you can act as an educational role model for your child. Here are just a few:

∗ **If you did well at school** – Make it clear to your children that you're proud of what you achieved at school and how useful it was to you later on. More importantly, tell them how much you enjoyed school and learning new things and your enthusiasm will rub off on them. BUT – and this a big but – be careful not to put too much pressure on them.

∗ **Take a course or learn a new skill** – When was the last time you learnt something new?

sometimes children might be reluctant to tell you, so try simply saying, 'tell me something I don't know' (meant honestly, of course…). If you've ever watched a child playing with a younger sibling or friend, you'll notice that they enjoy teaching and explaining things as much as they do learning, but they don't get the chance to do it very often. This interaction is also a great opportunity for children to feel that their relationship with their parents works both ways.

## Different learning styles suit different children

Time for a little psychology… There is a well-established theory that says that almost all of us respond best to one of three styles of learning. The evidence seems to be that whichever category we fall into is innate – we're like that from birth – and so this model also applies to children:

**Visual learning** (through what is seen)
∗   This style appears to be the one that most people respond to, as around 65 per cent of the population, or two in three people, learn this way.
∗   This approach teaches using written information, notes, diagrams and pictures.
∗   A person who learns best this way will also learn well using TV programmes and videos.

**Auditory learning** (through what is heard)
∗   Most successful for around 30 per cent of the population, or one in three people.
∗   People responding to this method learn best through what they hear – particularly by talking and listening.
∗   Someone who learns in an auditory way will like both quiet study and lively discussions.

Perhaps you'd like to do a basic course in a language, or learn to play a musical instrument? Perhaps there's something you've always wanted to do, like ride a horse or know how a car engine works? It's not too late, so take a home-learning course, or perhaps an evening course, and show your children that learning is always valuable and worthwhile.
∗   **Take an interest in what your children learn** – Talk to your children at least once a week about what they've been learning in school. This might seem an obvious thing to do, and

'I haven't been to school for nearly 20 years – how can I be a good example to my children when it comes to education?'

**Kinaesthetic learning** (through touch, movement and space)

✱ This is quite a rare response – only around five per cent of the population or one in 20 people prefer to learn this way. As the smallest group, it can often be disadvantaged by formal education.

✱ These people learn best through physical activity, imitation and practice.

✱ A common trait of someone who learns this way is to enjoy tinkering with things (both objects and concepts), in order to understand them better.

What all this means is that your child will probably respond best to learning information that is presented in one of these three styles. You don't have to be a child psychologist to analyze this; simply watch them carefully over the years as they develop their learning styles, and before long it should be fairly clear which approach suits them. Once you know this, you can support your child's learning by helping them to learn in the way that is most helpful to them.

**Did you know?**

It seems obvious, but it's amazing how often it's missed: two of the most common causes of learning difficulties in young children are problems with vision and hearing, and very often neither of these are diagnosed for months or even years into a child's education. Bear in mind, too, that many children don't know what their eyes and ears ought to be capable of, or if they are aware that they have a problem with seeing or hearing, they might be too embarrassed to tell anyone about it.

If your child is struggling with learning, either at home or in the classroom, having their eyes and ears tested should be one of your first ports of call (if this hasn't already been seen to within the last six months).

## Reading

Most children learn to read at some point between the ages of four and seven. Just as with all sorts of other skills, the arrival of this developmental milestone varies greatly, and this is not necessarily indicative of their intelligence. If your child seems to be taking longer to learn to read than their friends or classmates, don't panic, and don't assume that this is going to be the pattern for the rest of their education.

If you are keen to get your child reading, there are loads of things you can do to help them along; both before they start school and during the early school years. Familiarity and interest in language starts literally from birth – babies love being talked to, sung to and read to. Repetition is also helpful, too, and babies and small children love the familiarity of hearing the same story, poem or song over and over again.

Remember, too, that words don't just belong in books. Words are everywhere – on TV, posters, signposts and in shops, to name just a few places. From the earliest possible opportunity, encourage any interest your child shows in words – both while they're in the home and out and about.

## How schools teach reading

There are, in fact, three separate methods by which children are taught to read at school. In the past, individual teachers and schools tended to focus on just one of these methods, but over time it became apparent that a combination of the three was the most effective strategy. Check with your child's teacher which method they are using, it can be very disruptive if you start to teach your child at home using a different method.

These are the three methods by which reading is most commonly taught. (Note that

## Get them riveted by reading

The Department for Education have given out some great tips on encouraging early interest in words and reading:

* Play I-Spy – an excellent game to demonstrate to children that certain words begin with certain letters.
* At the shops, point out the different names of foods as you go past them – even if the word isn't written on a label.
* Let your child choose their favourite book and read it to them as often as possible. Apart from helping them with language, reading to children can also be a great way of getting them to sleep.
* Early on, show your child that words go from left to right on a page and then down to the next line, by following the words with a finger as you read them.
* Don't keep children guessing for too long about how to say a word – say it slowly, pronouncing each set of letters one at a time, before gradually saying it quicker.
* Don't be afraid to let your children develop their own reading style – slow and careful or faster and not worrying about mistakes. Children read differently, just as adults do.

the 'At home' sections are exercises that you can help your child with as soon as they are ready – typically from age two upwards.)

## 1   Look and say

This is the simplest of the three methods. The child is encouraged to learn whole words without breaking them down into syllables or groups of consonants. The core skill is 'whole word recognition' – meaning that the child memorizes the shape of the word – and it works well early on for important words. One problem with this method is that it doesn't teach the child any patterns that can be applied to new words, which means that every word must be learnt individually.

At home: Make small paper signs with the name of an object on them, and stick them to that object – such as 'chair' or 'table'. For really important words, like your child's name, write it on a card, mix it with other words on cards, and get your child to pick out their name.

## 2   Phonics

Phonics teaches children sounds that are made by syllables and clusters of letters, as well as the rules underlying these sounds. Firstly, the child is taught a very simple word like 'cat', then other words are introduced with the same sounds – like 'hat', 'rat', and 'mat'. The idea is that by repeating words with the same sounds and groups of letters, children can apply the rule they have learnt to new words with the same group of letters as and when they encounter them. Phonics are very effective for most children, but are particularly successful with dyslexic or slower-reading children, who tend to rely on sounds to learn to read.

At home: Say single-letter sounds (for example, 't t t t t') and get your child to repeat them. Also,

try playing basic games of I-Spy – but only with uncomplicated words that have a simple first consonant.

## 3   Whole language

This method is the one that relies most on the child's ability to improvise. Children are taught whole language by being given simple texts or books to read, based on previous experiences of language which are often picked up using 'Look and say' and 'Phonics'. This approach requires the child to have the confidence to try a word, and sometimes even guess it. Pictures are often used and through them the child is taught to 'read' the story. Although difficult, it's perhaps the best way to encourage more advanced readers.

At home: Read a favourite book to your child and try getting them to finish a phrase that they know well, such as 'Once upon a...'. Encourage your child to learn nursery rhymes and simple poems off by heart.

# Dyslexia

The word 'dyslexia' comes from the Greek language and means 'difficulty with words'. For all the myths that surround it, that really is the simplest way to describe the condition. Dyslexia is caused by a difference (as opposed to a defect) in the area of the brain that deals with language, which affects the basic mental skills needed for learning to read, write and spell. Psychologists have shown that dyslexic people process information differently to non-dyslexics.

Though dyslexia is very common, as with ADHD there is not a crystal-clear boundary between those with the condition and those without it – it's less 'black and white', and more 'shades of grey'. But the British Dyslexia Association believes that around four per cent of the population is severely dyslexic and a further six per cent have mild to moderate problems with words.

Dyslexia occurs in people from all backgrounds and of all abilities; from people who cannot read to those with university degrees. It can emerge or be diagnosed at any point during a child's education and, increasingly often, in adulthood. The most common signs of dyslexia are:

* Difficulty with reading, despite average or high intelligence in other areas.
* Difficulty with sequences, for example, problems with getting dates in order.
* Erratic spelling.
* Poor organization or time management.
* Difficulty organizing thoughts clearly.

Dyslexic people of all ages can learn effectively, but they may need to be taught using different approaches. Dyslexia is no reflection of the IQ of the child, or of their performance in school.

Dyslexia is a puzzling mix of both difficulties and strengths. Dyslexic people often have distinctive talents that non-dyslexics don't have, like excellent problem-solving and creativity, as well as some or all of the usual difficulties. Dyslexics who have been very successful in later life include Agatha Christie, Albert Einstein, Richard Branson, Felicity Kendall, Steven Redgrave, Benjamin Zephaniah and Robbie Williams.

Having a label doesn't actually make that much difference to the child, it's just that they are going to need a little extra help.

Finally, the same also applies to dyslexia as with ADHD with regard to labelling. If your child is diagnosed with dyslexia, it's really important not to get too fixated with the label. Your child is still normal, with his or her own unique talents and personality, like any other child. With your help, they can adapt to the condition and still fulfil all their potential to become successful, happy adults.

For more information, a great place to start is the British Dyslexia Association (BDA) – go to http://www.bda-dyslexia.org.uk or call their helpline on 0118 966 8271.

**Did you know?**

In the last 20 years, psychologists have identified a condition that is similar to dyslexia, but the problem occurs with numbers, rather than words. It's the rather awkwardly-named dyscalculia.

Children with dyscalculia show many of the equivalent symptoms to dyslexia, such as getting numbers the wrong way round, but they might also have more trouble with mental and written arithmetic than would be expected for their intelligence. If this seems the case with your child, it might be worth talking to a specialist to develop strategies for helping your child with their maths. Later in life dyscalculia shows up in poor timekeeping and an inability to keep track of money.

To find out more, start with this useful article on the BBC's website. http://www.bbc.co.uk/skillswise/tutors/expertcolumn/dyscalculia/

# Hot topic **ADHD**

## What is ADHD?

If you have school-age children, it's likely that you've heard of a condition known as ADHD. It stands for Attention Deficit/Hyperactivity Disorder. Although it affects both children and adults, nowadays it is usually diagnosed in childhood. It is characterized by poor concentration, impulsiveness (frequently acting on sudden whims), overactivity (higher than normal energy and activity levels), distractibility (easily distracted) and a lack of inhibition with people they don't know. At school the child seems unable to sit still and stay quiet for more than a few moments, and as a result they often disturb others. But ADHD isn't a disease or illness like measles – there is no simple, black and white boundary between those who have it and those who don't.

There is evidence that ADHD is at least partially genetic, but it has also been associated with difficulties in upbringing; including a lack of clear boundaries, or a lack of attention from parents. A combination of genetic factors and difficulties in upbringing can often lead to a diagnosis of ADHD, however, some children have such a genetic vulnerability that they would develop ADHD even with 'perfect' parenting.

Although there is broad agreement that ADHD is a real condition, experts disagree on how many children are actually affected by it. Current estimates are anywhere between one in 20 and one in 50 children, and boys are three times more likely than girls to be diagnosed.

ADHD can affect language development and learning to read. The learning difficulties resulting from ADHD can be challenging enough, but the other reason why ADHD is a concern for both parents and educationalists is that it can contribute to a wide range of other behavioural and social problems. Children with ADHD often suffer emotional difficulties because they aren't like their peers, and their school marks tend to be lower than average. It can be very frustrating not to be able to do something their classmates take for granted, such as reading a page in a book.

The good news is that many children with ADHD go on to do well in later life. It's possible that it is the nature of schooling alone that ADHD children struggle with, as opposed to the much greater variety of skills required in life outside school.

## How to detect it

Diagnosing ADHD is a complicated and skilled process and all of the symptoms mentioned at the top of this passage should be assessed by experienced child psychologists before a judgement is made. Even if you think you recognize some of the tell-tale signs in your child, it doesn't necessarily mean they have ADHD.

When children are getting lower academic results than their intelligence suggests they should be achieving, some parents look to ADHD as an explanation for a problem that might actually be being caused by other factors, such as

boredom, poor sleep patterns or emotional difficulties. A wrong diagnosis of ADHD can seriously harm a child's development, particularly when the real answers may actually be more simple and closer to home.

## How can parents help?

There's a great deal that parents themselves can do to reduce the problems associated with ADHD, but in a minority of cases professional help is also needed. Behavioural treatment is usually the first port of call and parents will be advised on how to make changes to the way that they care for their children in the home environment – including their approach to sleep, diet, exercise and interaction with their children. These changes very often bring about an improvement, but in rare cases drugs, including Ritalin, can be offered by a psychiatrist or paediatrician.

Whether or not you use drugs is entirely your decision, and you do have the right to refuse if you are uncomfortable with the idea. There is strong evidence that Ritalin and other drugs improve the

concentration of children with ADHD, but they aren't a complete cure, and most psychologists agree that they should be used as a last resort. There can also be side effects – these are rarely serious, but they are unpleasant enough to ensure that these drugs are not handed out in minor cases.

## Living with ADHD

Finally, and most importantly – if your child is diagnosed with ADHD, it's vitally important that you don't become concerned with the label and let it change how you feel about your child. They are still talented and unique, and with your help your child can adapt to the condition, often overcoming it completely, and live a normal, happy and successful life. There are many celebrities with ADHD whose condition has not hampered their ambitions, these include Daniel Bedingfield, Tom Cruise, Jim Carrey, Billy Connolly and Whoopi Goldberg.

For more information, contact the National Attention Deficit Disorder Information and Support Service, or ADDISS. Go to www.addiss.co.uk or call 020 8906 9068.

## Qualifications

There is far more to a good education than just coming out with a set of qualifications. When it comes to jobs and careers, there's an unfortunate truth about qualifications: they tend to be forgotten almost as soon as you start your first real job. Nine out of ten employers will tell you that they consider work experience to be far more important than academic qualifications.

But, rightly or wrongly, qualifications still play a very important part in determining career prospects because they make one really major difference – they help you get the job in the first place. The majority of employers will say that, although qualifications don't count for very much once you're in, they are used as a sort of filter for determining who the employer might be interested in taking on, and who they aren't.

One of the most important things for parents to bear in mind when it comes to qualifications is that they truly aren't the be all and end all. Whatever you were expecting – if your child doesn't get many GCSEs, or perhaps gets lower grades at A Level than they were hoping for – you must keep calm. Your children will always look to you for a reaction to their achievements, and if you start to panic and think your child will never get a job or get into university, this will rub off on them. You need to gently coax your children into thinking optimistically and confidently about their future, even if there are setbacks along the way.

### Exam anxiety

If you went to school in the 1970s or 1980s, you'll clearly remember that fearful time of the year – exams. It was when, for a few weeks, it seemed like a huge amount of pressure was riding on just a handful of exams which lasted an hour or two each. A minority of us seemed to actually enjoy this period – working under pressure was an exciting challenge – but for most of us it was very stressful and seemed a little unfair when two or even three years' work would be assessed in just a couple of hours.

In the 1990s, coursework became a significant part of the testing system and by the mid-90s, around 15 per cent of the overall GCSE and A Level result was decided by coursework. Today this change has gone even further and the coursework is now worth around 30 per cent.

What this means is that children can be assessed on work that they've done throughout the school period, which means that it's fairer and they don't have to feel that everything rides on the exams. If you child tends to get anxious under pressure, it's a good idea for them to choose subjects that mean more coursework and less exams, if that option is available.

## Girls and boys

The academic performance of girls at school has increased enormously over the last 20 years, and much more so than the performance of boys. A study in the US of 900 primary school children in 2002 revealed trends that have also been observed in the UK:

* Girls performed better in school subjects including English, Maths and Humanities, whereas boys achieved higher results in Science.
* Girls worried more than boys about how well they did in school.
* Boys were less concerned about academic performance than girls, particularly if they failed, so tended not to be disappointed by bad results.

There are all sorts of theories as to why girls are now doing so much better in school. Some people believe that girls are inherently better suited to classroom learning than boys, while others think that in mixed schools, girls are more able to concentrate in the presence of the opposite sex than boys. But one factor that has almost certainly been important is the greater aspirations that girls now harbour for having careers, and that both parents and teachers have for them.

The increase in girls' performance and engagement in education continues right through the system. In 1970, only one in three university students in the UK were female, whereas nowadays that figure is up where it should be – to around 50 per cent. So it's obvious that today the opportunities are there for girls at all stages of the education system in this country.

## Did you know?

The recommended guidelines for the amount of time children in the UK should spend on homework are:
Age 5-6: 1 hour a week
Age 7-8: 1-1.5 hours a week
Age 9-10: 30 minutes a day
Age 11-12: 45-90 minutes a day
Age 13: 1-2 hours a day
Age 14-15: 1-2 hours a day
These figures are more than for some countries, but lower than others. In the UK, homework tends to start earlier in life than for children of other countries, but older UK children seem to do less than in other countries.

## Homework

Unsurprisingly, research into the homework habits of children at secondary school confirms what we would expect – that for children over the age of 11, those who do their homework regularly perform better academically. But, interestingly, there is no consistent evidence that homework improves the performance of primary school children.

So why should really young children be made to do homework? In the view of the current government there's one overriding reason – that at that early stage homework strengthens the link between what happens at school and what happens at home and thereby encourages active involvement by the parents in their children's education.

But if homework can be such a chore, why do children have to do it anyway? Why isn't there a nice, simple divide between home and school life? Couldn't children just stay on after school to do their extra work, and then come home and relax? These questions seem fair enough, but there is one excellent reason as to why children are asked to do homework at home: it's about teaching them to take responsibility for their own learning. If children only ever study when they have a teacher breathing down their neck, then they don't learn to motivate and discipline themselves to work independently.

A child's reluctance to do homework is very common and so, once again, you have an important part to play in how your child thinks about homework. With the right help from you, homework can become a simple, straightforward part of a child's daily life – and even something they enjoy doing. Three factors really help to make this happen – routine, environment and support.

## Routine

It's exactly that – ensuring that your children knuckle down to their homework at a similar time each day, and early enough that they don't get tired halfway through. The best time for this tends to be early evening. Let your children have a nice break of an hour or so after school, then settle them down for homework. Try and make sure there is a set routine for homework at the weekend too. Very often homework is left until Sunday night, but most children enjoy their weekends more if they get it out of the way on Saturday and don't have it hanging over them.

## Environment

This simply means the place and the conditions under which homework gets done. There are a few basic principles that should be observed as closely as possible:

* Firstly, they should do their homework in a room that is pleasant to be in; quiet, well-lit and with as few distractions as possible. Children's bedrooms are not usually the best idea as they tend to be full of toys and posters, so getting

them to work in a dining room or a study are better options.

* Secondly, TV and music should not be allowed under any circumstances while homework is going on. Children will protest until the cows come home that they can work with music in the background – but all of the scientific evidence suggests that, with the exception of quiet classical music, this isn't the case.

* Finally, friends and siblings doing homework together can actually improve their work, but this needs careful monitoring. Children can really motivate each other to get on with it and share ideas, but don't leave them alone to work in a room where they can chat and distract each other, unless you're certain they can be trusted to concentrate.

## Support

This is where you can really make a difference. As I said before, research shows clearly that the amount of involvement parents have in their child's learning and education strongly predicts their later academic performance. So:

✱ Guide them, but don't do the work for them – if your child asks for your help, you'll have to strike a careful balance. On the one hand, answer any questions that will help their broad understanding of a subject if you can, but on the other, don't give them the complete answer to any question that they've been set – they might get a good mark, but they won't know why. Both you and their teachers need to have a clear picture of how well they understand what they're being taught and this picture will become blurred if you are effectively doing their work for them – even though it might be tempting to help them out at times.

✱ In longer assignments that involve research, help your child in any way possible to get access to the sources they need. Take them to a library, show them useful sites on the internet and invest in books for them if it will help.

✱ Take any opportunity you can to praise both high achievement and real effort. If your child is performing well in a subject, that's something to be encouraged, but it's equally important to commend perseverance with a subject or task that your child finds difficult. Make sure you reward effort rather than natural talent: if your child finds a particular subject very easy, don't reward them for a mark or exam result unless they've genuinely worked hard to get it.

✱ Just as with work during school time, children need to understand the relevance of a piece of work to their own lives: they need to know how the task relates to the rest of their learning, and why the work is valuable for them in the future.

✱ Keep homework in perspective: it's valuable, but there is more to your child's learning and development than just sitting at a desk for hours on end, poring over textbooks.

# Kris' Top Tips

✱ Get involved with their schooling.
✱ Encourage them to LOVE learning.
✱ Remember that academic results, while important, are not the be all and end all of your child's education.
✱ Help them to get their homework done by creating routine and the right environment, and by giving them your support.
✱ Lead by example and learn something new yourself.
✱ Show your children how to use the computer safely. If you don't have one, consider buying one.
✱ Have their eyes and ears tested every two years.
✱ Help their reading as much as possible – but be patient.
✱ Be aware of learning differences, including dyslexia and ADHD, but don't allow them to influence how you think about your child and their future.
✱ Children learn best in different ways. Present them with books and information in different styles, and play to their strengths.

## Computers

In a society where increasingly IT skills are essential rather than just a bonus, children should be encouraged to learn computer skills from as early an age as possible. Homework is a great way for them to learn the basics, so if you don't have a computer at home, it's well worth investing in one.

Computers make invaluable homework aids in many ways, but these are two of the most important:

* The internet contains a vast amount of information that can help with homework. There's lots of material available from trustworthy sources such as the Department of Education and the BBC, but also enormous amounts of information on particular subjects that can be found by using search engines. This way of learning encourages children to follow their particular curiosities about a subject, rather than stick to what is in the school textbook.

If you are concerned about harmful internet content, there are numerous programmes available that enable you to restrict what your children can access to certain sites. Start at www. thinkuknow.co.uk for more details.

* Word Processing – this is a basic package for writing text that comes with most computers, such as Microsoft Word or WordPerfect. Once a child becomes a proficient typist, they'll find that they can do homework much quicker on a computer than they can with pen and paper. The other really big advantage with word processing for homework is that it is easier for children (and adults!) to edit, change, re-write and experiment with their work before they hand it in at school. This encourages them to think through what they are communicating, and how they communicate it.

**reading**

Michelle and Quentin Hammond have two boys – Bradley and Joseph. The family as a whole was addicted to television and every room in the house – apart from the bathroom – had a TV in it. It appeared that Bradley alone was watching an incredible 45 hours every week, and most of it was unmonitored by his parents.

One of the biggest health problems facing these two boys was an almost total lack of interests beyond watching television and playing computer games. When Kris met up with the family for the first time, neither of the boys had ever read a book, so one of the golden rules Kris set for the family was that Bradley and Joseph should visit the library.

Kris explained to the family that children who do better at school and are more active learners end up with more possibilities in their lives; they tend to be happier and healthier, they earn more money and have better career prospects. For Bradley and Joseph to start reading, after

# Case Study **The Hammonds**

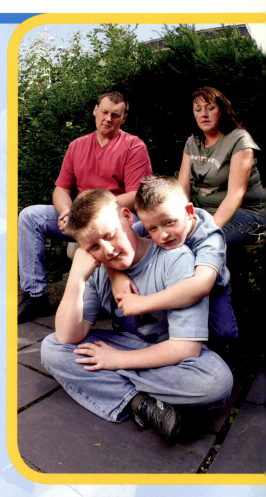

thinking it was something on a par with going to the dentist, Michelle and Quentin needed to make some time to devote to it. By allocating 15 to 30 minutes every night to reading the parents could show the boys that it's an important activity, and something they should value and commit to. Each weekend Quentin was to take Bradley and Joseph to the library to choose a book for the week. Kris hoped that this way the family would get into the habit of reading, and come to enjoy it.

In addition, Kris felt that it was vital for the Hammonds, and particularly Bradley and Joseph, to reduce the amount of television that they watched each week. Kris set the family a new viewing allowance of two hours in front of the box each day and all other spare time would be spent in academic or social activities. The many televisions around the house were reduced to just one, which Michelle could more easily supervise.

So with fewer televisions to distract them, the children have turned to other things to occupy themselves instead. Reading and enjoying books has now become a firm fixture in the Hammond household.

# 5

# Love and praise

Can you love your children too much? Previous generations believed withholding affection strengthened a child's character, preparing him or her for the realities of life. Today we know the opposite to be true: the more love you show your children, the better adjusted they become. However, it is *how* you show love that makes the difference…

# Getting involved

Playing a part, supporting, guiding, communicating and learning enables parents to understand how their children are developing, and makes children feel their parents are interested in them. Sounds simple, but nowadays it seems there are increasing pressures on us to cram more into our already busy lives, and it can be hard to make family time.

## Why is getting involved so important?

**We've mentioned this before, so why devote a whole chapter to it? Simple; it's because it is the most important factor in your child's psychological development. How well you are involved with your child, has a very strong bearing on their mental health, how well adjusted they are, and their long-term happiness. This is true whether your child is three months old, three years old or thirteen.**

## How does this involvement affect your child?

Children with involved parents will typically:

* Perform better in school.
* Feel better about themselves.
* Be less likely to develop emotional problems.
* Be less likely to take risks and get into trouble.

Getting involved is about much more than just asking your child questions about things. Most parents are familiar with the way that conversations with children of any age (and not just teenagers...) can sometimes turn into interrogations:

| | |
|---|---|
| You: | How was school today, Jamie? |
| Your child: | It was OK. |
| You: | What lessons did you have? |
| Your child: | Maths and French. |
| You: | Did you pass that tables test? |
| Your child: | Yep. |
| You: | Did you hear that Robbie Williams has learnt to fly just by flapping his arms up and down? |
| Your child: | Nope. |

[Pause...]

| | |
|---|---|
| Your child: | Er... What's for tea, Mum? |

At times, getting children to open up on just about any subject can be difficult, or verging on the impossible. Remember that children tend to carefully choose their moments to open up, just as adults do. You might not know when those moments will be, but the more involved you are in your child's life, the more likely it is that you'll be there when it happens.

# What does 'getting involved' really mean?

The simplest answer is to do the following exercise:

1   Firstly, write a list of all of the activities that your child takes part in where you don't know exactly what they do in that time. Be honest with yourself – the list is for your benefit only. Here are some possible examples:
* Lessons at school.
* Activities after school.
* Homework.
* Playing with friends.
* TV and computer games.
* Books they're reading.

Now, once you've finished, take a careful look at that list. If you're surprised at just how much your child does that you know little or nothing about, don't make yourself feel bad – you're in exactly the same boat as most parents.

However, now is the time to do something about it. For every one of the activities listed above, ask yourself two questions:
* How you can find out more about what's involved?
* How can you play a part in it?

2   Next, make a similar list that includes how your child thinks and feels about all the major parts of their life. Again, just write down the things that you really don't know much about – and be honest – such as:
* How happy they are at home.
* How happy they are at school.
* How they feel about themselves.
* If they feel they have enough friends and people to play with.
* How they feel about their family (you included).
* What they are interested in, or would like to try.

Then, for each of these areas, think about how to best talk to them about it.

N.B. One important point; remember that children – especially older ones – need privacy just like adults. Give them space, and don't make them feel like you're spying on them.

## Being involved – how it changes over time

The way we involve ourselves in our childrens' lives should change steadily and constantly over the years. Up to the age of three or four years old, much of our involvement is about carefully controlling an activity to make sure that it is safe and enjoyable for the child. But as he or she gets older, parents find that they can 'relax the reins' a little more as children start to understand safe ways to do things. All of this could apply to homework, play or learning a new skill. When a child turns into a teenager these reins must be relaxed a little more – to the extent that the child can really begin to experiment and find things out for themselves, as well as learn to take responsibility for situations when their parents aren't in control.

There's an important principle behind all of this. 'Relaxing the reins', which is a necessary and healthy part of allowing your child to grow up and be more independent, does not mean 'not being involved'. Many parents think that the best way to let children learn as they get older is simply to leave them to it. This approach is OK in small doses, but there should never be a time when you are not involved at all in your child's life.

## Making time – and guarding it carefully

The majority of parents would say that they lead busy lives; there isn't a lot of spare time for a start, and we often feel as though it's a struggle to fit everything in. Lots of activities (both practical and enjoyable) get rushed as we try to get to our next commitment on time.

Something else happens when parents are busy, too. We *multitask*: we feed the baby while we're on hold to the electricity company, or we have a bath while she's asleep. Later on we might grab something to eat in between going to the supermarket and doing the school run, or we sneak a quick nap while our children are watching their favourite DVD. We multitask because it saves us valuable time, but multitasking has a downside, too. When we're so used

## How to allocate and guard time with your children

✳ 'Fence off' time with your children hours, days or even weeks in advance.

✳ Treat that time with the same commitment that you would a meeting at work or something equally important. Mark it in your diary if necessary.

✳ Tell friends, family and work about it if you have to, to make sure they know you can't be anywhere else but home at that time.

✳ Turn off your mobile and turn on the answerphone. Don't let calls distract you from your children – except in genuine, serious emergencies.

✳ *Work does not count as an emergency* – unless you work for the emergency services. If once every few months you have to rearrange a family outing for work, that's OK, but more often than that and perhaps you need to rethink your priorities.

✳ Working from home is increasingly common. The fact that your whole life is in one place makes it harder to draw a clear boundary between work and family life. *Be rigid* about what is work time and what is family time.

to doing two things at once, we can easily forget that there are times when we need to give our full attention to our children.

A perfect example of this is setting aside time for an activity with your children – usually in the evenings and weekends. If you don't give your full attention to that activity, children are surprisingly good at picking up on it. This has two consequences – firstly, your child doesn't enjoy the activity as much (because they're not really interacting with you), and secondly, they feel disappointed that what they thought was going to be 'family time' is being eroded. As a general rule, don't be tempted to fool your children into thinking that they have your full attention when they don't. Multitasking is an unavoidable fact of life at times, but children can often sense when we're not totally focused on them. If we try to conceal this, our children find it confusing and disappointing when they realize the truth – and ultimately they can lose faith in us.

child time

## Working parents

One of the commonest obstacles to getting involved that parents face is work.

In most families, one or both parents have to work. Research shows that children whose mothers work full-time during the first five years of their children's lives tend to perform less well at school and are more likely to be unemployed or experience psychological distress in early adulthood. These patterns are more likely to affect boys than girls, but are less likely to occur in children of mothers who work part-time. *This doesn't mean that mums shouldn't work full-time.* In many families, and particularly in single-parent ones, mums don't have a choice. However, it does mean that often there is a price to pay for spending less time with your children when they are very young and that you should consider this carefully if you're planning to have children and work full-time. On the upside, children who attend nurseries or other childcare under the age of five are often more socially confident, as they have had to learn to be more self reliant.

If you are a working parent, and your employer is pressuring you to work hours that leave you with no family time, *you can do something about it*:

* Talk to your employer: tell him or her about the time pressure you're under and how it is adversely affecting your family life. Despite the longer hours that many of us work these days, most employers are sympathetic to the demands of family life.

* The law states that employers must offer flexible working wherever possible, and it is becoming an accepted practice in many organizations. It may mean keeping the same overall hours but at different times, or reducing your hours along with your pay, or working from home for a certain number of days a month.

### Spending time with your children – quality not quantity?

It's a thorny question. In the late 1980s a parenting approach referred to as 'quality time' became increasingly popular. This idea began in the US but it has recently been widely adopted in the UK. What this theory suggested was that it was OK to spend less time with your children, as long as what time you *did* spend with them was *quality time*. This seemed to suggest that somehow certain activities or ways of interacting with your children were more valuable than others, and as long as you filled your time together with those 'quality' activities, everything would be fine.

Essentially, this theory has become popular because of the increasing work demands on parents in both the US and the UK. Most western countries work longer hours, have lower unemployment rates and have more women working than ever before. (This is probably truer of the UK than almost any other country in the world.) The pressure on parents to juggle work life and family life

# Hot topic **Quality time**

has never been greater, and so the quality time idea was attractive to many parents because it seemed to say that they shouldn't feel guilty about spending less time with their children.

So does the quality time theory hold any truth? Well it does in one sense: two people (whether parent and child, or two adults or two children) can spend hours or even days in each other's company without really interacting, communicating, learning about each other or being involved in each other's lives. What happens during that time is the important thing. BUT – and it's an important but – there is a limit to how much any relationship, and particularly a parent-child relationship, can be compressed into short bouts of 'quality time'. This extra pressure can in fact cause more harm than good.

One strong argument for increasing the quantity of time spent with your child is because this is a particularly important factor when it comes to communication. As we pointed out earlier, children on the whole don't like feeling pressurized to communicate – they like to take their time, and choose their moments carefully to say what's on their minds. The only way to make sure that you're there for them to talk to is by spending a quantity of time with them.

So the long and short of it is that it is equally important to devote a sufficient *quantity* of time to interacting with your children – you can't simply make up for a lack of quantity by increasing quality.

## Other ways of getting involved with your child's school

There are LOADS of ways that you can get involved with your child's school. On the whole, schools appreciate all the help and involvement that they can get from parents, so try and make a little time to join in on some of the following:

### Open evenings

A good way to find out more about what's happening in the school – and they can often be relaxed and fun occasions.

### Plays and concerts

If your child is in a school play or concert, make every possible effort to be there, as it usually means a lot to your child.

### Sports days

These events can be great fun and, again, if your child is competing do make every effort to be there. Sports days are often during the day so they can be harder for working parents to attend, but it's a really fun, sociable day out when you can also chat to both their teachers and other parents.

### Helping out on school trips

Many schools welcome parents along on school trips to help out as an extra pair of responsible hands. It might mean a trip to a farm, a museum, or later on perhaps the theatre. You'll usually have a great day out yourself, as well as contributing to it for the children.

### Governors' meetings

These are a good place to raise any concerns that you might have about the way the school is being run (as opposed to specific issues you may have regarding your own children), as well as finding about any major changes that might be happening in your school, such as amalgamations, curriculum changes and relocations.

### Parent-Teacher Associations (PTA)

Although PTAs don't usually have formal powers, they're one of the best options you have for finding out about what's really going on in your children's schools. You'll be able to discuss issues and problems with both parents and teachers, and often in a setting that enables you to have your say in a way that wouldn't be possible at a more formal event.

## Getting involved with your children's social group

This doesn't mean following your child around every second of the day, but as a parent you have a responsibility to show an interest in your child's social life and be aware of how they spend their leisure time.  This isn't because parents should be constantly checking up on their children but it can help to prevent your child getting into trouble as a result of having friends who are a bad influence. Your child will choose his or her own friends.  Peers

# Kris' Top Tips

gentle questions, but don't pressure them.

✱ Get as deeply involved with your child's school as you can. Attend all evenings to discuss your child's academic performance, and pop along to PTA and Governors' meetings if you have time.

✱ If your child's school has a home-school agreement, take it seriously. It's a good checklist for being involved with your children's education, and will tell you what you have a right to expect from the school.

✱ Maintain a strict distinction between work time and family time.

✱ If you are your child's main carer, investigate all your options before working full-time and try to find a balance between work and home life.

✱ As your children grow up they'll want more freedom and more privacy. This does not mean that you should stop being involved in their lives.

✱ Take time out for yourself. It'll make you a calmer and happier parent.

✱ There's no substitute for spending a good *quantity* of time with your children.

✱ Mark out some time for your children and don't let distractions get in the way.

✱ If there are areas of your children's lives you feel you know little about, make it your goal to find out. Ask are important and influential in your child's life, and by the time they reach secondary school your children will probably be spending more time with their friends than with you. You cannot choose your child's friendship group (much as we'd like to at times) and you can't tell your child what to think, but you can make a big difference to how much your child will be influenced by those peers. Children who have an open and warm relationship with their parents will feel more able to discuss problems that arise which will also make them less likely to succumb to negative peer pressure. Later on in this book you will find a chapter about communicatio; this is the best way to ensure that your child has the emotional tools to deal with any unwanted peer pressure or risky situations.

It's also important to try and limit the amount of unstructured times your children spend out with their friends – chances are it will be spent roaming the streets or gathering in groups, neither of which are conducive to good behaviour. As a general rule, always try to follow the 'three Ws' rule – know who they are with, where they are, and when they'll be back. That way, you can relax knowing that your child is safe and your child has enough freedom to grow and develop as an independent person.

## Make time for yourself, too

After everything we've said about spending more time with your children, it might seem a strange piece of advice to give – but keeping time aside for both you and your partner is a critical part of parenting.

* No parent needs to be told that bringing up children is stressful. We all need time that is ours to control – a little space in which to unwind

and to do the things that makes us happy as individuals, rather than as parents. If we are happy in ourselves, we are happier parents.

* Relationships need regular attention to stay healthy. Make sure that at least once a week you and your partner spend time together without the children. Any expense that you incur (such as a babysitter) is worth every penny. A happy, healthy relationship makes for a better set of parents.

* Absence makes the heart grow fonder – and in measured quantities this is absolutely true. Spending time apart from your children can make you miss them and look forward to seeing them that little bit more. Your children will feel the same way too, as having an occasional short break from their parents reminds them how much you do for them and how much they love you.

Try not to think of time away from the children as a luxury – it's a necessity. This doesn't mean leaving your children to fend for themselves for large stretches of time, but it does mean being kind to yourself and finding a way to relieve the pressure that family life can create.

# Case Study **Getting involved**

In several of the families that Kris worked with, the parents were often tired and overworked, and simply weren't finding the time and energy to have fun with their children – more often it was a case of letting them amuse themselves with the TV or games machines while they got on with other things.

One of the golden rules that Kris used with these families was instituting Family Fun Days. The idea behind this was to get the family to regularly spend a whole day together doing something they all enjoyed – and something that, where possible, would also be stimulating and educational.

The Applebys, for example, spent a day together in Edinburgh at a brilliant photography workshop, where the family got to see how their family photos were taken and printed. The Reynolds, although a close-knit family, had a son, Michael, who was finding that as a result of his poor diet and lack of exercise, he was losing confidence rapidly. Kris used the Family Fun Days to give Michael a say in how the family enjoyed themselves. As a result, Michael began to feel he had more input and involvement in the family, which boosted his confidence and gave him a sense of control over his own life.

In families such as the Hammonds and the Swains, where there was more than one child, the children still got to choose what they did on Family Fun Days, but they had to take it in turns to choose what they did.

In all of the families the Family Fun Day proved to be one of the activities that had the most positive effect on many other issues such as discipline, communication and respect. In itself, this clearly shows the value of spending proper time with your children.

# 7

# Discipline and boundaries

Talk to ten different parents and you'll get ten different views about discipline. At one end of the scale you have parents who believe that smacking is the only way, and at the other end, you'll find mums and dads who set few boundaries and let their offspring do as they please. We all want our children to behave well, so who has got it right?

## Why boundaries are important

**The first thing to say about discipline is that it *is* important. Children need to be loved – most parents agree on that – but they also need boundaries. Many parents are reluctant to enforce discipline because they don't want to be unpopular with their children, particularly if they remember the discipline they received in childhood and feel that it was unnecessary or harmful.**

**The reality is that all children need boundaries, and if they cross over these boundaries then they need to be disciplined. As adults we may think that the idea of living by rules and limits is unpleasant, but the truth is that children need and thrive on boundaries. They need to know what behaviour is acceptable and what is not and this kind of moral structure, far from making a child feel uncomfortable, actually makes them feel secure. In the same way that routines make children feel safe and protected, so clearly defined boundaries help your child to make sense of the world.**

As an adult you need to be able to control your own behaviour. In all social interactions we have unwritten rules about what's appropriate and what's not. Adults who have not learned the rules and limits of social behaviour find interacting with others problematic. People who are very impulsive, demanding or aggressive, for example, often find that they don't relate to others and find it difficult to form friendships or relationships.

Children learn these boundaries as they grow up. As a parent, your job is to set and enforce these rules so that, as your children become more independent, they can start to develop their own sense of internal control. By the time they are teenagers, the role of imposing control has gradually moved from you to the children themselves. For example, a young child needs to be told to wash and brush their hair every day, whereas a teenager will do this for themselves without being asked (hopefully!). So, rather than harming your child, by setting boundaries and imposing discipline you are actually helping them to become an independent, well-adjusted adult.

### 'No' and 'Because I said so!'

So, why do we have to learn to say no to our children? It can seem cruel to deny your child something that they want, and no-one likes to be the bad guy, but no is a useful word and one that is essential for good discipline. You need to say no to your child at a young age so that later in life he or she can say no to his or herself. If you can't say no to yourself as an adult, your life will be driven by whim and impulse and you will find it difficult to delay gratification; falling victim to the 'I want it now' syndrome.

Although no is a negative word, it can be used to teach your child positive lessons. It's a powerful word, however, so it's important to learn how to use it properly. The key is to strike a balance: if all your child hears is the word no, it can be very frustrating and dispiriting for them. However, if their day is full of yes's, then the first time they hear no it will come as a great shock and you're guaranteed to have a battle on your hands. In reality, the world is full of both no's and yes's, so you need to reach a compromise.

If you find yourself constantly saying no at home, it might be worth changing your environment and taking your child somewhere where it's easier to say yes. If you are worried about your child hurting themselves at home when they are playing, for example, take them to a soft play centre where they can experience greater freedom and you can enjoy giving them that freedom, without worry.

One of the problems with no is that it offers little explanation as to why a certain behaviour is not allowed. Rather than using the ubiquitous 'because I said so' as an explanation (which tells your child you don't really have a good reason for it), if you can explain your decision, do. Children are naturally inquisitive and will want to know why something is forbidden, so you are much more likely to get your children to comply if they understand what you're trying to accomplish. If you can't think of a good explanation, or your child is using endless 'why's?' to delay doing what he is told, then it's ok to say, 'Because you will be making me happy if you do so'.

## Case Study **The Applebys**

In the Appleby household, eight-year-old Amy was running the show. She got what she wanted, when she wanted it. Used to getting her own way with everything, Amy was also quick to throw a tantrum if things didn't go according to her plans. Unfortunately, parents Darren and Kate were loath to be tough on her and as a result, not only was Amy failing to learn the importance of boundaries and discipline, but she was also suffering from an over-indulgent diet. The fact that her mum and dad never said no to any of Amy's requests for junk food and sweets meant that Amy had ballooned to six stone and was already classified as clinically obese. The Appleby's were literally killing their daughter with kindness.

So what did Kris recommend? She pointed out to Darren and Kate that children benefit from boundaries and that children need to learn their place in the world to help them develop a real sense of security and stability. By learning to say no to Amy, Darren and Kate would be helping their daughter develop her own internal controls and independence. Children of Amy's age can change very quickly and even quite ingrained behaviours can be modified in just a few weeks.

Learning to say no to Amy has been a struggle for her parents, with Darren having more success at standing firm than Kate. However, despite this they have managed to set some good boundaries for their daughter and have had great success with changing her diet and encouraging her to look after herself and her teeth.

**no sweets**

## Why children break boundaries

So, we know why boundaries are important, but this doesn't prevent children from attempting to break them. Children, just like adults, like to get their own way. You are bound to have rules and limits your child doesn't like: he or she might not like the fact that they have to go to bed at certain time, or that they need to do their homework instead of going out and socialising. Children lack the life experience and foresight to really understand the benefit of some of life's boundaries. They might enjoy staying up late every night, for example, but do they really understand the consequences of being constantly tired at school? Similarly, schoolwork might be a drag but the repercussions of letting your child drop out of the school system can be very damaging in the long term.

As a child grows up and becomes more independent, they will develop ways of doing things that differ from your own and they will most likely have different views from you on all manner of topics. A degree of conflict between parents and children is inevitable and is a normal part of family life. Studies have shown that the things parents and children argue most about are household chores, homework, appearance and social life. Rather than try to get rid of conflict all together (which is practically impossible), the best thing a parent can do is to equip themselves with tools to deal conflict when it happens. Before we look at how to handle conflict, however, we need to look at the different styles of parenting and what effects they have on children.

# What's your parenting style?

The amount of conflict and disobedience in a household can be predicted by observing the parents' relationship with their children. The type of parenting style that exists in a family can have a profound effect on how the children behave. Over the years, psychologists have identified four broad styles of parenting – which tend to remain consistent throughout the child's life and with any subsequent children. The four different styles of parenting are based on how much the parents try to control the child (also called 'parental demandingness'), and how much they listen to what their child wants ('parental responsiveness').

**Parental demandingness** is also called behavioural control. It sounds scary but it simply means supervising children, setting boundaries and being prepared to discipline them when they misbehave.

**Parental responsiveness** means being attuned to their needs, being supportive and being prepared to modify rules as your child moves from one stage to another.

The four styles of parenting that have been identified show different levels of demandingness and responsiveness. The four styles are:

## Authoritarian

We've all probably met or heard of someone who is an authoritarian parent. These adults tend to be very demanding, focused on obedience and expect their orders to be obeyed without quibble. This rather old-fashioned style of raising children is also characterized by the parent not responding to what the child wants or to any nuances in a situation.

This is the 'do as I say, no questions asked' school of parenting. As punishment authoritarian parents often use emotional control – making the child feel guilty or ashamed – or a physical punishment, such as smacking. This sounds extreme, but it is still a *very* common form of parenting.

## Indulgent

This approach is at the opposite end of the scale from the authoritarian parent; indulgent parents demand very little in terms of behaviour but they are highly responsive to what their children want. These adults tend to accommodate their child's every whim, often in the belief that saying yes to everything is the best way to show their children that they love them. Boundaries and limits are few and far between – indulgent parents tend to let their children do what they please and rarely punish them.

## Uninvolved

This type of parent is both undemanding and unresponsive; they don't ask anything of their children and they don't give anything in return – no control, no punishments. Uninvolved parents can appear not to care about their children, and in extreme cases they can even be neglectful.

## Authoritative

These parents are both demanding and responsive to their child's wants: they set clear boundaries for their child to follow, but they also listen to their child's wishes. Authoritative parents have no problem in asserting their will when necessary, but they are also open to compromise or rule changing if the situation demands it. These parents will act if a rule is broken but it tends not to be in the form of emotional control fare worst of all; children whose parents are neither demanding nor responsive are most likely to perform badly in all areas. The benefits of authoritative parenting and the negative effects of uninvolved parenting can be seen as early as the pre-school years and can carry on right through adolescence into adulthood.

or physical punishment. In this style of parenting, rewards are used to encourage and reinforce good behaviour (see below).

### Which style of parenting works best?

Studies have shown that the last style of parenting on this list – authoritative parenting – generally seems to be the most successful. Because the child feels listened to, while understanding that there are clear boundaries in place, this type of parenting tends to reduce conflict between parent and child and also helps to establish trust and respect on both sides. Children of authoritative parents also seem to be more socially competent and do better at school, even at an early age.

Children of very strict authoritarian parents, on the other hand, tend to perform moderately well in school and avoid getting into trouble, but they are also more likely to have poorer social skills, self-esteem problems and higher levels of depression. Children from indulgent families tend to be exactly the opposite – they usually have good self-esteem but often perform badly at school and are more likely to get involved with problem behaviour. Those with uninvolved parents

## Getting children to behave

So we can see that a good two-way relationship between parent and child is the foundation for encouraging good behaviour, but how does this translate into every day life and what do you do when children break rules, as they invariably do?

### Encourage good behaviour

We all want well-behaved children who know the difference between right and wrong. Numerous studies have shown that the best way to achieve this is through the use of positive discipline, without having to resort to punishments that hurt a child either physically or emotionally.

Too many theories on discipline rely on the assumption that children are inherently naughty and that the relationship between parent and child is a constant battle of wills. Positive discipline, on the other hand, assumes that there is a loving relationship between child and parent, that children like and want to behave well, and that good behaviour is expected and rewarded.

Children behave at their best when they understand what constitutes good behaviour and why it is important, so rewarding good behaviour helps motivate them to keep on trying. This is the 'carrot' in the carrot and stick analogy. Believe it or not, children like to please their parents and the trick is to spot when your child is behaving well and to acknowledge it immediately. Rewarding good behaviour as soon as it happens will help to reinforce it and make your child feel good about themselves. It doesn't have to be anything major, it can be a small thing such as your child clearing away the table without asking or putting away their toys. The reward can be anything – spoken praise such as, 'great job' or, 'well done', a hug or kiss, a treat – but the main thing is that your child knows that he or she did a good thing. Younger children often like rewards, such as an extra bedtime story or eating their favourite meal, while older children might respond better to earning points towards a special toy or a trip out.

## Punishing bad behaviour

At the same time, you do need to punish bad behaviour when it happens. The two most effective methods are 'time out' and removing privileges (for example, docking pocket money or being grounded). We shall look at physical punishment and verbal abuse later on in the chapter, but suffice to say that both these approaches are ineffective at best and downright dangerous at worst.

In any type of punishment, three basic factors are key: first, that the punishment should be directly related to a specific act of misbehaviour, not just because you feel your child is generally naughty; second, that it should be age-appropriate; and third, that you should be consistent.

# Kids love rewards!

| Not all rewards for good behaviour have to be material ones. Try to mix and match social rewards (such as smiles and hugs) and fun activities (such as going to the cinema) with the material treats (such as extra pocket money or a toy). Here are a few ideas to get you started: | Social rewards | Fun activities | Gifts and treats |
|---|---|---|---|
| | Hug | Cinema visit | Extra pocket money |
| | Smile | Trip to the park | Points towards a bigger treat |
| | Wink | Baking or cooking | Favourite meal or dessert |
| | Clapping hands | Staying up 30 minutes later | CD or book |
| | Verbal praise | Having a friend to tea or for a sleep-over | Toy or game |

# Make a reward board

Reward boards or star charts are a great way to motivate young children to behave well. They work because they help children to clearly see the effects and results of good behaviour.

## Get creative!

You can make your own reward board at home. Be as creative as you like and get the children involved too – the more glitter, paint and colours the better! The picture can be anything you like, but the key is to have ten boxes or circles somewhere in the design that can be filled with a sticker every time your child behaves well. You could draw ten bubbles, ten presents, ten rungs on a ladder or ten smiley faces, for example. Even better, make them have a destination – it could be ten footsteps towards a treasure chest or ten steps to the top of a princess's tower. Once you've designed it, you'll also need to buy a couple of packets of stickers – the brighter the better. Every time your child behaves well they get a sticker on the reward board. When they have earned all ten stickers, your child gets a reward.

## How to use your reward board

✳   Decide on the behaviour you'd like to change (for example, tidying their bedroom or helping around the house). Choose only one behaviour at a time.

✳   Show your child the reward board and explain how it works. Make it clear which behaviour you want changed and which you are rewarding, for example, 'You get a star because you tidied your room so nicely – well done!'

✳   Put the reward board somewhere very visible – the kitchen wall is ideal.

✳   When you put a sticker on the board be very positive and celebrate the event with lots of verbal praise.

✳   Never take stickers away. If your child misbehaves and doesn't receive a sticker for a while they will see that they are not getting any closer to their reward target.

### 'Time out'

'Time out' involves removing your child from an activity or a group and putting them on their own for a short period. Choose a time out place that is free from distractions without being frightening for your child – the corner of a quiet room, a chair or the bottom stair are good options – and call it the time out place.

* When your child misbehaves, kneel down to their level, look them in the eye and tell them calmly but firmly that the behaviour they have just displayed is unacceptable. Warn them that they will have to sit in the time out place if they continue to behave like that.

* If your child continues to misbehave, calmly take them to the time out area. As a rule, your child should sit on their time out spot for no longer than one minute for every year of their age – for example, four minutes for a four-year-old.

* Stay within sight or earshot of your child, but don't get into a discussion with them.

* If your child gets up before time is over, sit them back down and start the time out from the beginning.

* When the time out is over, explain clearly why they were given a time out and ask them to say sorry. Hug them and then let them leave the time out spot.

* Amongst pre-school children time outs have been shown to increase compliance with parental wishes by a factor of three, and they continue to be useful as your child grows up. Once your children reach their teens, however, time outs might not be the most appropriate

method of punishing bad behaviour and removal of privileges can be more effective.

### Removal of privileges

This method of punishing bad behaviour works with children of all ages. Removal of privileges involves withdrawing an activity or facility that the child values, such as going out with friends, pocket money or watching the TV. The removal of privileges teaches a child that his or her actions have consequences and this helps them to take responsibility for their own actions and to think before they act.

The most effective way of removing privileges is to make the punishment relate directly to the misbehaviour. For example, if your teenager insists on staying out late with her friends, even though you have told her you'd like her back at a certain time, then the best removal of privilege would be to stop her going out with her friends for a while. A different example might be removing a favourite toy if your child refuses to tidy up her toys or play nicely with them.

When you remove privileges you should make sure that they are ones that matter to your child – there's no point docking pocket money, for example, from a child who has a part-time job and earns his own money. Equally, sending a child to his room might not be considered much of a punishment if the bedroom is filled with entertainment such as a computer and a TV. And finally, removing privileges works best if it's only for a short period of time – if children feel that they

**Did you know?**

A 2004 survey of 630 parents across Britain found that the most popular method of disciplining children was the removal of privileges. Hard smacking was the least popular.

Source: YouGov

are never going to get a confiscated item back, they will give up on trying to behave well to get it.

## What doesn't work

People discipline their children in lots of different ways. If your children are behaving themselves then surely it doesn't matter which approach you use? Well, not entirely. Research has shown that some types of discipline, such as physical punishment and verbal abuse, although somewhat effective in the very short term, don't actually work in the long term. On top of that, these type of harsh punishments can have lasting consequences for both child and parent.

## Physical punishment

While physical punishment certainly has an effect on children, it might not necessarily be the one that you were hoping for. Years of research have shown that physical punishment, such as smacking, spanking or hitting your child, has a marked effect on children's behaviour, and not for the better. Children who are physically punished learn that hitting someone is an acceptable method of problem solving. Physical punishment is also a significant factor in the development of violent behaviour in childhood and later life.

The effects are the same wherever you go in the world. A global research team recently studied 336 families across six countries – China, India, Italy, Kenya, the Philippines and Thailand – and found that smacking resulted in more behavioural problems in all countries. All the children who were disciplined by smacking showed higher levels of aggression, anxiety and other emotional problems than their contemporaries. Children who are disciplined by corporal punishment are also more likely to go on to be bullies at school

and use aggression as a means of problem solving. Children who are aggressive then go on to find it difficult to integrate with children of their own age, are more likely to get involved in problem behaviour and develop conduct issues at school.

Some parents believe that physical punishments, such as a slap, work because they instantly stop the behaviour. This might be true, but physical punishments don't offer any long-term solution or teach the child why certain behaviour is inappropriate.

Furthermore, physical punishment is also a risky strategy for disciplining your child because it can get out of control and you could end up harming your child. It can be difficult to control your anger in a moment of crisis and sometimes parents find that they have unintentionally gone too far, whereas other parents find that they need to smack harder and harder over time in order to produce the same result from their children. Hospitals often see cases of what happens when smacking gets out of control and results in more serious harm, such as ruptured eardrums, brain damage and injuries from falls caused by blows. At its extreme end, the devastating statistic is that at least one child every week dies at the hands of their parents or carers in the UK as a result of physical punishment.

Given that there are other more effective strategies for disciplining your children, such as time outs or removal of privileges, isn't it better that you don't take such a risk with your child's wellbeing?

## Verbal abuse

Parents can often resort to screaming and shouting to get their children to behave. While we can all lose our tempers now and again, using verbal abuse as a regular strategy for discipline can have just as many negative impacts as physical punishments. In fact, children who are regularly verbally abused by their parents can go on to suffer a whole range of problems, including apathy, depression, hostility, concentration problems and eating disorders. Just because the child isn't physically harmed doesn't mean that they don't get hurt.

However, not only does verbal abuse cause harm to children, but it actually doesn't work very well as a method of discipline. This is for two reasons: firstly, because in order to behave well your child needs to believe that you have his or her best interests at heart, and secondly, the

## Hot topic **Smacking and the law**

The law on hitting children has recently been changed; while adults are not allowed to hit each other, a parent is still allowed to mildly smack a child and call it 'reasonable chastisement'. Although it is against the law for teachers, nursery workers and childcare workers to smack another person's child, anyone employed privately by a parent, such as a babysitter or a nanny, may smack a child as long as the parent gives permission to do so. Whoever is doing the smacking, however, may face up to five years in prison if any punishment causes visible bruising, grazes, scratches, minor swellings or cuts.

Most children's organizations, such as the NSPCC, believe that smacking should be banned entirely and in most other European countries, including Sweden, Germany, Italy, Denmark and Austria, children have the same legal rights as adults and there is no defence of 'reasonable chastisement'. But rather than get into the morals of whether smacking should be allowed or not, the primary reason not to smack is that it doesn't work. Research into child behaviour indicates that smacking is not a good way of teaching children the difference between right and wrong. In fact, children who are physically punished are more likely to respond with worsening behaviour or by becoming aggressive. Parents who describe their relationship with their child as less warm and involved are more likely to use smacking as a punishment, and evidence indicates that smacked children are more likely to behave aggressively in later life.

### Did you know?
Hitting children hurts parents, too. In 2002 the NSPCC asked parents what they thought about smacking and the results showed that most parents felt bad after hitting their children — around three quarters of parents said they felt upset, sad, regretful and/or guilty afterwards.

message that you are trying to convey is often lost when you shout and scream.

Children behave best when they feel that you like them for who they are. (See the importance of making a child feel loved in Chapter 5.) Successful parents are those who have children who believe that mum and dad care about their wellbeing above everything else. Children from this type of background trust that the decisions that are made on their behalf (even if they don't like them) come from parents whose intention is to love and protect them. If you constantly shout, scream, humiliate or name-call, then your child will soon doubt whether you have his or her best interests at heart. If your child thinks that you don't care, why should he or she follow your rules?

Equally important to bear in mind is that when you try to get something across in an angry way it is very easy to be distracted by the tone of voice rather than the content of the message. You might be absolutely right to tell your child that homework is important, but if this message is delivered in an aggressive, hostile way, your child will fail to see your point and only feel scared or angry in response.

Parents often react to this point and say that it is important to be firm. Yes, being convincing and clear about what you want is very important, but, in truth, that happens best when you are calm and controlled, not when you are ranting and raving. Being firm is not the same as being aggressive. You often find that parents are verbally abusive to their children in a moment of anger, and not because they deliberately want to hurt them. If you tend to let words out before you've had chance to calm down, take stock and think about what you want to say. Almost all of us could use a little anger management.

## Managing anger

All children have the potential to try your patience – it's what they do. You are in a hurry to get somewhere and your child is refusing to cooperate; you're in the supermarket and they have screamed the entire way round; they've broken your favourite vase even after you told them to be careful – it's normal to get angry from time to time. However, it's also important to control this anger and calm down before you discipline your child.

When you feel yourself getting angry the first thing to do is take a deep breath. Count to five slowly or repeat a calm word such as 'relax' to help dissipate any angry feelings and let your heartbeat slow. If necessary, take a time out for yourself and come back to the situation once you've calmed down.

However, if you feel that anger is a real problem in your family relationships you should consider asking for help from a family counsellor or try attending anger management classes. Your GP will be able to put you in touch with local counselling services, many of which specialise in family problems and dealing with anger.

Regular exercise also helps to maintain a sense of calm, as do relaxation exercises and yoga, and meditation will help to release tension in a controlled, healthy way. Diet also plays a part in anger as hunger can trigger feelings of irritability, and so too can excess caffeine and alcohol. Drinking alcohol will also lower your inhibitions, making you quick to anger and to behave more violently.

# Kris' Top Tips

### * Understand that boundaries are important

Far from being cruel to your children, setting boundaries helps them feel secure and safe in the world.

### * Accept that children will break boundaries

Don't feel disappointed if your children occasionally don't do what you asked them; children are always developing and growing as people, and testing boundaries is one of the ways we learn. All families experience conflict.

### * Be authoritative

Being too strict or too indulgent with your children isn't doing them any favours in the long term. However, try to balance exerting control with being responsive to their needs.

### * Be a parent, not a best friend

Sometimes your desire to be popular with your child will be at odds with your obligation to be a good parent – the latter should always win out.

### * Practise positive parenting

Children are born with a natural desire to please their parents. Rewarding good behaviour and viewing your children as good people is much better than ruling them with an iron rod.

### * Use reward boards

Let children see the results of their good behaviour – they'll soon work out that it pays to behave!

### * Don't use physical punishment or verbal abuse

Time outs and removal of privileges are the best ways to discipline your child when they misbehave. Negative punishments have poor results and detrimental long terms effects on both parents and children.

### * Learn to control your anger

Cut out the yelling and shouting and chances are that your child's behaviour will improve almost immediately.

### * It's OK to say no

Saying no is an important part of discipline. However, use it carefully and sparingly if you don't want its effect to wear off.

### * Avoid saying 'Because I said so'

Children will respect and comply with your decisions more easily if they can see the reasoning behind them.

# Case Study **The Reynolds**

**manage anger**

Parents often unknowingly pass on their anger to their children by being unable to control their own feelings. Mum Alma needed to learn to manage her frustrations because son Michael was learning from them. The pair also fought regularly, with Michael copying his mother's volatile reactions. By showing Alma that displaying anger is not positive behaviour and by changing her way of handling frustration, Kris encouraged her to lead by example.

An anger management therapist helped Alma to see that she needed to break the cycle of getting into fights with Michael and try to make him understand that she's the boss. Michael had learned that it paid off to keep arguing with his mother as often she would eventually give in, even if everyone ended up feeling angry and frustrated. To stop this pattern, Alma needed to see herself as the adult and Michael as the child – not her equal fighting partner.

The art of relaxation was also a skill that Kris thought both Alma and Michael would benefit from and one that they could use when emotions were beginning to rule their actions.

Within only a few weeks things quietened down a lot as both mum and son learnt alternative ways of resolving feelings.

As a result of this soul searching and learning how to deal with her own frustration and anger, Alma has changed her behaviour towards her son, and as a result the rows have lessened between them and brought a more harmonious atmosphere to their home.

# 8

# Respect and responsibility

This is where children get a pretty bad press. If you believe the media, discipline in schools is now at an all-time low. If children are so much more badly behaved than in previous generations, then who is to blame – the parents or the children themselves? How can parents teach children respect for others and the basic principles of good behaviour?

## Children and the media

A 2004 poll conducted by MORI turned up some very interesting findings about how children are perceived by the media. MORI combed through 600 of the most recent newspaper articles about young people, identifying whether the article was broadly positive, negative or neutral about them.

* More than 70 per cent of the articles portrayed young people in a negative light.
* In tabloid newspapers, 82 per cent of articles were negative.
* Only 13 per cent of all articles portrayed young people in a positive light.
* Around 30 per cent of all pieces about young people were about violent crime or anti-social behaviour.

These were extraordinary findings from one of the most respected independent bodies in the UK. They show that the media is very good at portraying the worst sides of young people. But why is this? Perhaps it is because such stories make for more sensational news, or perhaps because they simply reflect what the public thinks of young people. However, the most important question is one that the survey *can't* answer. To what extent is the media's view of young people correct?

Well, let's use the example with the most basic of statisics – crime. Most crime is not committed by young people. In 2000, 88 per cent of detected crime was committed by over-18s, and most of those were over 21s; but that's not a statistic you will often see reported.

## Anti-social behaviour

Anti-social behaviour is the term applied to a huge range of activities, of which children are responsible for only a small proportion – the vast majority of anti-social acts are committed by adults. Both local and central government are vague about exactly what anti-social behaviour is. This vagueness is partly deliberate – it enables local authorities to identify certain acts and behaviours as anti-social that may not be covered by a specific criminal act.

### Did you know?

The minimum age at which a child can be held legally responsible for a crime is ten years old. Around one in 50 children will at some point be formally reprimanded or convicted of a crime. However, children cannot be given custodial sentences until they are 12.

# Hot topic **ASBOs**

ASBOs (Anti-Social Behaviour Orders) are designed to prevent behaviour that causes disruption and unhappiness in the offender's community, such as theft, intimidation, drunkenness and violence. An ASBO can be given to anyone over the age of ten, and nearly half of those issued are given to children. They are aimed at preventing acts that are serious and persistent, but relatively 'low-level'.

Though ASBOs have been around since 1999, numbers have been rising steadily every year. In 2004, 2,652 ASBOs were given in England and Wales, of which 1,069 were given to children – around 40 per cent.

ASBOs were introduced for a number of reasons:

* They often deal with activities that aren't covered by a specific law, and so allow local authorities to stop behaviour or incidents that might otherwise go unchallenged.
* They are considered less harmful to a child's long-term development and life prospects than a jail sentence or time spent in a young offenders' institution. They also allow families the chance to modify behaviour in the home environment.
* From the point of view of the government and local authorities, they're cheaper to handle and enforce than custodial sentences.

An ASBO lasts for a minimum of two years, but has no maximum period. They very often include geographical restrictions on where a person can go unescorted, but they may also include a ban on a specific activity, such as swearing in public. A curfew may also be part of the ASBO, where the offender is banned from leaving their house after a stated time in the evening. In some cases an ASBO can also prevent the offender from spending time with certain other people, such as friends and acquaintances.

Although ASBOs are handled and enforced by police, they are in fact civil orders rather than criminal ones. However, breaches of ASBOs can be punishable by up to five years' imprisonment. Although young people are usually protected by anonymity in law, they are often named in the ASBOs as an alert to the local community.

Opinion is divided over whether ASBOs are too tough on children, or too soft. On the one hand it seems odd that behaviour that isn't considered a criminal act can, through breach of an ASBO, lead to a prison sentence. Many also object to the 'labelling' of children as antisocial that occurs by 'naming and shaming'. On the other hand, some feel that ASBOs are not a sufficient deterrent for children, as there is no custodial sentence unless the order is breached.

## Respect

When we talk about children and respect, we're often talking about the lack of it – particularly in relation to their elders. There is much debate about whether children really do have less respect for adults than they used to, but as a parent this argument is something of a 'red herring'. Children, like adults, need to respect everyone – not just parents, teachers and other adults but other children and, of course, themselves. But what does respect really mean?

Respect isn't easy to define, and has many different components. If you were writing a list of every single rule of respect that children should follow, you'd have an incredibly long list. There would be a rule for everything from what to do when standing at a bus stop next to a pregnant woman, to what to say when a friend tells you his mum and dad are getting a divorce. In fact, it'd take so long to write the list that you'd never get round to explaining these rules to your children.

Parents just don't have time to teach their children how to behave respectfully in every possible situation that they might encounter. So, what's the alternative? *Super-principles*. These are rules that children can apply to all situations and, if followed, should lead to a happy outcome. These are especially important in a situation where the child doesn't know which specific behaviour they should be adopting.

In terms of children showing respect, regardless of who it is directed at, the super-principle is simple:

**respect mum**

*Children should treat others as they themselves would like to be treated.*

But what should children respect? Here are the most important things:

### Property

Both yours and that of others. Property is important to all of us, but not just because we like to own nice things. For many people, property also has an emotional value, and is one way that we can express our individual tastes and interests.

A good way to teach your children to respect property is to let them have personal possessions from an early age that are theirs and theirs alone, then show your child that you yourself respect their things and their feelings towards them.

## Their environment

Here we mean their surroundings – their bedroom, their home, their street, their school, their town, and so on. In the society that we live in today, private property tends to get valued higher than public spaces – but children need to be taught to respect public places, regardless of whether they appear to 'belong' to somebody or not. 'Public property', such as bus stops, shopping centres or schools, belong to us all. For that reason vandalism and littering, no matter how petty, affects everybody who uses that space.

## Feelings

Again, it might be yours, or those of your friends or siblings. Empathy is the really important principle here. From as early as possible, children should be encouraged to put themselves in the shoes of others. When a situation arises, carefully explain to your child the feelings and sensitivities of the person involved and encourage your child to empathise with the person and what they are experiencing. Ask your child to think about how they would like to be treated in such a situation, and suggest that they behave in that way towards the other person.

## Privacy

Teaching children to respect privacy can be particularly challenging for parents. By the nature of the relationship, it's hard to give children as much privacy as you would demand for yourself. It's you that has to go into their rooms, tidy up, help them get dressed, and so on – not the other way round. Even so, the best way to encourage children to value your privacy (and that of others) is to help them have something that is private to them – a diary is ideal (and helpful in many other ways), or a safe box that contains precious belongings that only they have access to. This way, they'll understand how important privacy must be for others, too.

## Listening to others

Respecting the opinions of others is something that tends to be more important later in childhood, when children start to form opinions about things themselves. However, from a very early age you can teach your children to listen to what you and others have to say. How? Simple – by listening to them.

Don't cut over what they're saying if you can avoid it. It's *always* worth listening to what your child has to say on a subject, and take it seriously. You don't have to agree with them, but listening and considering their opinions sends them the message that what they have to say is important – not just in childhood, but in later life, too. If you don't respect your children's opinions, they will lose confidence in expressing them. And, above all, never forget that adults can learn from children too – not just the other way round.

## Physical space

Children need to learn as early as possible to respect someone else's body and physical space. This means not inflicting physical pain on others, or forcing others to do things they don't want to do. It also means not touching others in a sexual way that isn't wanted. None of this means that chidren can't play in a 'rough and tumble' way with each other, as almost all siblings and friends enjoy sometimes, it just means that rough play should only take place when all the participants are enjoying it, and no-one is likely to be harmed.

## Respect between you and your children

One shared concern amongst parents is that their children don't show them enough respect. This isn't a new worry – it is as common now as it was in previous generations. If there is a difference, it is that standards of respect are not the same today as they used to be. Some of this may be due to negative influences (such as the media), but for the most part it's a natural result of beneficial developments over the years, such as child protection laws and greater understanding of children's emotional needs.

Children are born with an innate desire to look up to their parents and be like them. As they get older, they begin to understand what it is to be a rounded human being with flaws and faults – and this applies to their parents as much as anyone. This is a natural process, so don't be afraid to show your children that you aren't perfect. In time, they'll come to appreciate the truth much more than any illusion you create for them.

In the previous section, we talked about how important it was for children to treat others as they would like to be treated themselves. Exactly the same is true for you – show your child respect and you're much more likely to get it back in return. If you find yourself being disrespectful to your children, you should ask yourself how you lost your authority so that you needed to resort to that kind of approach. Shouting, saying rude or impolite things and bullying are not behaviours that you want your children to emulate. Some parents use these tactics to prove to their children that they are in charge, however, they are actually more detrimental to your position and shows simply that you are throwing your weight around and abusing your power as a parent.

## 'Talking back'

Parents, like anyone in authority, sometimes wish that their children would simply do as they're told, without questioning it. One of the examples of disrespect that parents say winds them up most is their children 'talking back' to them.

If you are already a parent, ask yourself for a moment how often you use one of these expressions:

* 'Don't talk back.'
* 'Because I said so.'
* 'You'll understand when you're older.'
* 'Don't argue with me.'
* 'Children should be seen and not heard.'

All parents have moments when there isn't time for discussions or arguments about something – it just has to get done. But none of the above expressions are necessary to get the point across. What we really mean when we say these things is, 'I expect you to just fall back and do exactly what I, or anyone older and stronger, tells you to do.' This isn't good for any child. Later in life, they'll feel as though they shouldn't question any decisions at all.

So what should parents do in this situation? The answer is to calmly explain why you've asked your child to do something, and why there is no alternative. Don't assume that your children won't understand your reasons, or that they need to be protected from 'adult reasoning'. In an absolute emergency, where no discussion is possible, of course it's OK to take action immediately, but it's very important that you explain as soon as you can after the situation why you had to act without explanation. The idea behind this approach is that you are making your children feel that they are allowed to know what's going on, and there is a reason for an action, even if it comes after the event. If you take time to do this, your children will trust you to do the right thing in future emergencies.

## Setting a good example

The old saying that 'charity begins at home' works for a lot of things, and this is certainly true for respect. As I've said before, the best way to teach children the value and importance of respect is to show them respect in the first place. Again, this is the principle of setting a good example. Children who are shown respect by their parents are much less likely to show disrespect to others. But what else do we mean here when we talk about respecting our children?

## Handling emotions

Children very often get emotional about things that adults don't – whether it's angry, afraid, or just upset. It's essential that parents take their children's emotions seriously, however irrational or over-sensitive they may seem. All parents face 'emergency' moments when they have to tell their children to calm down, or stop and think, but that does not mean that you should dismiss their feelings out of hand – always be sensitive to the situation.

**Honesty**

There are few things worse for children than when they are not believed about something, especially by someone as important as a parent. Almost all children lie occasionally (as do most adults) – this is a natural part of learning – but parents should never give up believing what their children tell them. It's better to let your child take you for a fool about something once, than to assume they are never telling the truth.

**Teach by example**

Another way to teach our children respect is to show them that we respect others. As with diet, exercise, learning and many other areas covered in this book, children learn a huge amount of their behaviour and attitudes from their parents. If they see you treating others with disrespect, or behaving selfishly in a situation where the considerations of others are important, they'll often do the same. Here are a few examples:

* **Out and about** – Do you pay attention to others? Do you treat staff in shops and public places with patience and respect?

* **Authority** – Do you demonstrate respect to figures of authority (such as police, teachers and doctors) through your behaviour and attitudes?

* **Examples from the media** – Do you show that you respect the opinions of people in the media, or do you dismiss what they say out of hand?

* **Respect for individual differences** – Do you show respect for people who differ from you – in race, religion, social class and opinions – or are you dismissive of them?

Responsible teaching by example can also help to avoid more serious situations arising. Research

suggests that certain types of negative parental behaviour can significantly increase the risk of their children turning to crime. Those types of behaviour are:

* **Neglect** – Where parents spend too little time with their children so they simply aren't aware of their children's misbehaviour.

* **Conflict** – Literally some form of conflict between a parent (or parents) and a child. It could be physical or emotional cruelty, or simply inconsistency, which undermines the respect a child has for their parents.

* **Deviant parental behaviour and attitudes** – This is all about the example that a parent sets for their child. If parents regularly display contempt for the law, or suggest in some way that law-breaking is acceptable, children are very likely to adopt the same attitude.

* **Disruption** – This is where family life is seriously disrupted, often because of conflict or even a separation between parents.

## Responsibility

Respect and responsibility are two sides of the same coin: giving responsibility tends to foster respect. The word 'responsibility' covers a very broad range of things. Of course, the need for children to take responsibility for their actions gets steadily greater as they get older, and by the time they are adults the hope is that they have become fully responsible and are will retain that attitude for the rest of their lives.

As for young children, here's something that many parents don't realise until too late: *children love responsibility*. Receiving responsibility shows trust and that they are being treated like a real person (as opposed to a 'half-person' who isn't capable of looking after themselves). It also prepares children for one of those hard but inescapable facts of life – that there are times when something will only happen if you make it happen.

Give your children responsibility from the earliest possible opportunity, under safe conditions. For example, let them:

* Feed a baby brother or sister.
* Wash the car.
* Walk the dog.
* Help with a simple part of a meal, such as washing vegetables or laying the table.
* Buy you something you need from the shops.
* Grow a plant for themselves, and look after it.

# Case Study **The Jacksons**

Teresa Jackson is a working mum from Leeds who lives with her two children, Shannon, who's ten, and Steffan, who's 11. When Kris met the family for the first time, the house was totally chaotic.

Things had become too much for poor Teresa, who had lost confidence and authority with her children and wasn't getting any respect from them. But rather than lay down lots of rules for the children, Kris stated that the real problem lay with Teresa's confidence. To help boost this, Teresa was taken off to do an extraordinary challenge – paragliding.

This single experience pushed the boundaries of what Teresa thought she could do and increased her confidence massively. This in turn enabled her children to develop a new-found respect for their mother.

Think of your child as someone who is capable of making a useful contribution to the running of the house. Remember, you're not just teaching them something, you're getting a free pair of hands! However, at the same time, if you are giving your children a new task or responsibility, follow these rules carefully:

* If at all possible, make it something *enjoyable*. If your children learn to enjoy responsibility first, you'll find it much easier to get them to knuckle down later to unpleasant tasks that have to get done.

* Make sure that all necessary safety measures are in place for the particular activity, relevant to their age.

* If possible, watch them doing something for the first time, but make it clear that you are only doing so to *help them get it right* – don't forget that children are very good at sensing whether their parents have confidence in them. If they get it wrong first time, don't give up, praise whatever it was about it they did right.

* As soon as they've got it right, *back off* and let them get on with it at every opportunity. 'Backing off' is a really important part of responsibility – it's a sign that you trust and believe in them.

* Unless it's an emergency, or they simply can't get the hang of something (perhaps because they are too young), don't get impatient and take over the task. This is a sure way to lose the value of the exercise.

## Independence and decision-making
So far in this section on responsibility I've talked about practical responsibilities, like doing a small job for you, or helping out with a sibling or even a pet. I've explained how this teaches your children to act independently, but there's also another important part of responsibility and independence – *decision-making*.

The principle here is just the same as for tasks. From as early as possible, allow your child to make decisions for themselves – as long as it is safe to do so – such as:

* If they're getting ready for an activity or a party, let them plan their preparation – how long it's going to take them, what they'll need to bring, what to wear, and so on. If they're way off, guide them, of course, but let them think it all through first.

* If they're having a friend over, let them decide what games to play and what they are going to do with the time.

* With a big piece of homework or a project at school, encourage your child to plan it carefully, and think through how to approach it.

It's not just about leaving a child to it; there are ways that you can help them make decisions responsibly. For example, in the case of the school project, get them to write down all of the possible angles from which they could approach it, and put a list of 'pros and cons' by each one. At the end, they can have a look at the list and see for themselves which approach will work best.

A little later on, if the family is going on a long walk or perhaps a cycle ride, ask your children to look at the map first and try to work out the best route. Once they've done it – and if you think it's a safe route – *take their advice*. This is, of course, the most important part of the exercise for a child – testing whether their decision worked in practice. If it does, they'll be chuffed to bits, and if it doesn't, they've learned some valuable lessons for next time.

These are just two examples of how to teach your children to make decisions for themselves, but there are opportunities to do this in just about every part of life – think about instances in your day-to-day routine or at special events that would get them to work something through the way an adult would.

## Bad influences

All parents, whether their children are six or 16, think that their children's peers are one of the biggest influences on their attitudes and behaviour – they might be friends from school, next-door neighbours, cousins or siblings. This response is hardly surprising, since the average secondary-school child spends twice as much time with their peers as they do with their parents. One of the most common worries that parents have as their children grow up is that the influence of these peers may turn out to be negative.

Your child's relationship with their peers is not just about pressure – children tend to seek out friends and acquaintances that they like or admire. In other words, it's about *peer preference*, not just *peer pressure*. Many parents, when faced with a

discipline problem that is either ongoing or even just a one-off event, will often quickly assume that it is their child's friends who are exerting pressure on them to behave badly, rather than exploring the possibility that their child is actively seeking out troublesome peers.

Recent research has thrown up some predictable findings, such as that children who socialise with smokers will be more likely to take up smoking. The same is true for drugs, alcohol and criminal behaviour. But the same research also shows that children usually seek out these particular peers, rather than being the victim of pressure from them.

When children are very young, you're likely to spend time with the families you get along with, rather than those that your children choose. But very soon (usually as soon as school begins), it becomes immensely hard for parents to influence who their child is friends with, and trying to control this is more likely to lead to rebellion than good behaviour. What parents can change, however, is how much their children are led by others.

This brings us nicely on to another of the 'super-principles' that I mentioned earlier. You can't expect to prepare your children for every new situation they'll ever encounter with their peers, but you can teach them this:

*Children must learn to make up their own minds.*

Children will always listen to what their peers have to say, but they should be encouraged to never act on the advice of peers without forming their own opinions first. For parents, the overall message is simple – focus your efforts on teaching your children to make good decisions for themselves, rather than worrying about what a bad influence their friends might be.

# Kris' Top Tips

✱ Respect is a two-way street. The best way to get your children to respect both you and others is to *show them respect In the first place.*

✱ Children should be taught to treat others as they themselves would like to be treated.

✱ Show respect to others. Don't forget what an important role model you are for your children. How you treat a sales assistant, for example, demonstrates to them how they should behave.

✱ If you want your children to trust your motives when you tell them to do something, explain to them why it should be done. If it's an emergency or there just isn't time to talk them through a situation, take action anyway, but explain as soon as you can after the event why that action was necessary.

✱ Children must learn to make up their own minds about things. You won't always be around to help them make responsible decisions.

✱ The more you try to seem like the perfect parent to your children, the harder it will be for them when they realize that you're not flawless.

✱ Give children responsibility from the earliest possible opportunity – but make sure that any necessary safety precautions are in place. This applies to tasks and decisions.

✱ Don't assume that friends or classmates are responsible for your child's bad behaviour. It is more likely that the child has sought out friends who behave a certain way than has been pressured into things.

✱ Children get a terrible press these days in terms of respect and responsibility. It's up to you to fight against that by believing in your children and trusting them as much as you can.

# Case Study **The Allcocks**

Lisa and Royston live in Birmingham with their four children – Michael, 13, Billie, seven, Kayce, six, and Lucy, four.

When Kris first met up with the Allcocks, their diet, and particularly that of the children, was extremely unhealthy. It wasn't just that they were eating a lot of junk food and excessive amounts of sugar and salt, but they also simply weren't aware of the importance of fruit and vegetables.

Rather than just telling the Allcocks to buy more fruit and veg, Kris decided to put matters into the children's hands too, and get them to take responsibility for their own diet and understand more about healthy eating. So, in week three, Kris's task for them was to plant a vegetable garden. With the help of garden makeover expert Eddie Campbell, the children were soon planting potatoes, carrots and peas, and taking the responsibility for watering and tending them.

Despite a low yield in their first season as gardeners, the Allcocks are full of enthusiasm for growing their own and have even decided to fence off a corner of the garden to keep as a permanent allotment!

# 9

# Safety

Throughout this book we've talked about providing an emotionally safe place for your children and the importance of providing a haven for them. But just as important as this is creating a safe physical environment. Ironically, sometimes the areas that parents worry about the most aren't always where the greatest risks lie.

## What parents worry about

**A specially commissioned MORI poll asked parents what worried them the most. Among the top forty answers were quite a lot of concerns about safety, and in particular parents seem to spend a great deal of time and energy worrying about:**

**\* Their child being abducted or murdered.**

**\* Their child being a victim of crime or physical violence.**

**\* Their child being hurt on a school trip.**

**\* Their child being injured in an accident at home.**

**\* Their child being knocked over by a vehicle.**

**To help parents to decide how concerned they should be about each of these problems, it's best to look at exactly *how likely* it is for each event to happen, *what would happen* if the worst did occur, and how much parents can do to *prevent it* happening in the first place. In other words, we need to understand the concept of risk.**

## Abduction and murder

If you believed everything that you read in the papers and watched on the TV, you'd be forgiven for thinking that the abduction and murder of children by strangers is a common event. As a result, many parents feel that they have no other choice but to keep their children indoors. This in turn means that, today, most British children have less physical freedom and independence than they did thirty years ago: far fewer play outside and enjoy the unmonitored play that their parents' generation did.

In reality, the likelihood of an individual child being taken by a stranger and killed is tiny – less than five out of sixteen million children per year – and while no amount of child murders is acceptable, we have to recognise that the number (less than ten children a year) is very small and shows no sign of rising. Compare that figure to the 100 or so children who are killed by vehicles each year, and that puts it into some kind of perspective.

It's also a common belief that girls are more likely to be murdered than boys, and so they experience even more restrictions in what they can do and where they can go. In fact, almost two-thirds of child murder victims are boys.

The depressing reality of these scenarios is that the majority of the children who are murdered each year are usually killed by their parents or close family members, not by strangers. Those at greatest risk are children under one year of age – a baby is five times more likely to be murdered than an older child. The strain of looking after a small infant is just too much for some parents, especially if they live in difficult circumstances such as extreme poverty or an abusive relationship. Women who suffer from severe post-natal depression are also at a greater risk of harming their children.

So where does this leave parents? How much should we worry? One conclusion is that rather than focusing on risks posed by random strangers, most families should turn their attention inwards and make sure they are creating a safe, violence-free environment for their children. Key to this is managing our own stress and frustrations, and getting help if we feel unable to cope.

Another thing we should take from all this is that parents who excessively restrict their children's freedom and opportunities for play because of worries about strangers are actually doing more harm than good. Children who are driven everywhere or prevented from exploring the outside world have fewer chances to develop their own independence, interact with peers, or be physically active. The less exercise they get, the greater their chance of developing obesity – the *real* health risk for children. Ironically, children who are also driven everywhere or who haven't had many opportunities to practice being a pedestrian are at a greater risk of being killed by a vehicle. And finally, on an emotional level, children brought up to believe that the outside world is a dangerous place will not have the confidence or social skills of a child who feels able to cope with new people and new situations.

## Physical violence and crime

We already know that a huge majority of the children murdered every year die at the hands of their parents or relatives. In the same way, 80 per cent of all violence that occurs against children in their home is committed by someone known to the child. Violence occurs in all sorts of households – from the richest to the poorest – but the statistics show that when it comes to serious or long-term violence, people who are under stress are most likely to commit the act. This stress often comes in families where one or both parents are unemployed, on a low income, young, managing by themselves or are part of an unusually large family. Fathers, step-fathers and father-substitutes are also twice as likely as natural mothers to be implicated in the abuse.

The real risk to your children in this instance is you – not strangers. If parents are the people most likely to harm their children, we need to ask ourselves whether we are creating the right environment for them and making sure that we are not resorting to physical abuse when we experience stress.

Physical punishment is also a large source of violence against children (see Discipline and boundaries, p131). Think about your approach to discipline: can you manage your anger? Are we setting a good example for our children? Teaching them that violence is an appropriate reaction to of falling off something – whether it's the stairs, a bed or a chair – while boys are slightly more likely to be involved in this type of incident than girls. Similar numbers of children are affected by other types of injuries as they are by falling. Swallowing or choking on a foreign body is the second most common cause of accidental home injury, with around 50,000 incidents every year. Around 35,000 children are hurt every year as a result of an accidental burn or a scald, with hot drinks causing the most number of injuries. A further 25,000 children (mostly under-fives) are treated every year for suspected poisoning – household items such as cleaning materials, medicines, alcohol and garden sprays are often to blame.

The most common form of fatal accident inside the home is a house fire, which, thankfully, claims much lower numbers than any of the other accidents. Even so, around 30 children die every year as a result of house fires.

From the age of seven, children spend a greater proportion of their time outside the home and as a result they are much more likely to have an accident away from mum and dad – this affects over a million children every year. Of these, accidents at school are surprisingly common, with around 350,000 children being injured during term time every year. Other 'hotspots' include playing fields and public playgrounds – around 180,000 children are injured while playing sport every year (ball sports being the most common cause of injury), while around 30,000 are injured at playgrounds.

Away from minor injuries, road accidents are the biggest single cause of serious injuries and deaths in children. In 2002, for example, around 35,000 children were hurt in accidents on the roads in the UK, with almost 5,000 of these being counted as serious accidents and with 200 actual fatalities.

## Surely accidents are part of growing up?

Well, yes and no. Children do need to explore their environment; only through play and trial and error do they learn which behaviours work and which don't. They also need to know how to deal with everyday risks such as crossing the road, using sharp objects or handling hot water. You cannot shield your child from every single challenge in life, and nor should you. There are also great benefits to participating in certain activities that carry a risk – sport is a good example of this, as any possible risks are outweighed by the health benefits many times over. But there is a great deal of difference between leaving children to their own devices and educating them as to how to cope with risk.

The sorts of accidents that children are involved in tend to relate very closely to their age. Babies and toddlers, for example, often have accidents as a result of falling, as they have yet to develop good balance and coordination. Very young children also surprise their parents by suddenly being able to do something which the previous day they couldn't. You often hear parents in accident and emergency departments telling doctors that they turned their back for one second and their baby suddenly learned how to crawl, walk or roll into a dangerous situation. That's why accidents such as babies rolling off beds or falling down unguarded stairs are so common. Children also lack the experience or foresight to see that a particular situation might be dangerous. *Understanding where your child is in his or her development is key to preventing accidents.*

**Did you know?**

A hot drink can still scald a baby fifteen minutes after it's been made.

Source: CAPT

# Hot topic **Risk-prone children**

A child's personality can also have a big impact on whether they're likely to be involved in accidents. Believe it or not, some children are naturally more risk-prone or excitement-seeking than others. In fact, this tendency can even be seen in as children as young as two. In the same way that thrill-seeking adults like new and exciting situations, so risk-prone children enjoy novel and stimulating experiences and are less averse to taking physical risks. Researchers even tested to see whether babies had risk-prone personalities or not, and they discovered that babies who are quicker to react to, and reach for, new toys are more likely to go on to be toddlers who are adventurous and highly exploratory.

If you do have a child who seems to have an excitement-seeking personality, firstly, don't worry. Risk-taking children have the benefit of being highly engaged with their surroundings and can go on to lead very stimulating, fulfilling lives. The only problem is that they are also likely to be involved in accidents and take part in anti-social behaviours. As a parent, the best thing you can do is to keep a close eye on their behaviour and make sure that they understand the basics of personal safety as soon as possible. You also need to check that their risk-prone tendencies don't put their siblings or peers in danger. Try channelling their energies into positive activities such as sport or drama, which will help them to avoid potentially harmful behaviours later in life, such as drug abuse or driving at high speed.

On a final note, children with Attention Deficit Hyperactivity Disorder (ADHD – see p82) can also display risk-prone behaviour. This can manifest itself in the child being very impulsive, distractible and disobedient, as well as seeking out constant excitement and stimulation. If you have any concerns about your child's behaviour and suspicions of ADHD, talk to your family doctor.

As a parent you need to tread a careful path between allowing your child the freedom to experiment and learn while also protecting them from unnecessary harm. Play and exploration are natural and highly important aspects of your child's development. By engaging with the world, children acquire crucial skills and judgement, so trying to insulate them from all risk is counter-productive in the long term. At the same time, while the odd bruise and scrape is part and parcel of being a child, you should always protect them from any unnecessary and potentially life-threatening accidents.

## Are some children more at risk than others?

Unfortunately, the answer to this is, yes. There are four main factors that affect how likely your child is to have an accident. The first is age. Children under five are the most likely to have an accident in the home, whereas this statistic declines in children between the ages of five and 15, when they are more likely to have an accident at school, play or on the roads. The second factor is the sex of your child – boys are roughly twice as likely to have an accident as girls. The third factor is your lifestyle. Children from poorer backgrounds tend to have more accidents than children from affluent families, often because many less well-off parents lack the resources to buy important safety equipment for their home or car. And the final factor, which is closely linked to lifestyle, is physical environment. Where you live can have a big impact on child safety. If children don't have a safe place to play – as is the case with many high-rise estates or communal buildings, or where there is a large volume of traffic – accidents are commonplace.

# Make your home safe

While it's totally impossible to shield your child from ever having an accident, you can make a significant difference to the chances of them injuring themselves at home. Consider the following:

## Falls

✳ Install safety gates at the top and bottom of stairs until the child is a confident walker.
✳ Fit safety catches on windows.
✳ Put corner guards on tables.
✳ Wipe up spills and tidy up any scattered toys.

✳ Never leave babies unattended on raised surfaces such as beds.
✳ Secure loose carpets.

## Burns and scalds

✳ Fit and regularly check smoke alarms.
✳ Have a fire extinguisher in the house.
✳ Don't smoke in the home.
✳ Keep matches and lighters out of reach.
✳ Use fireguards over gas or open fires.
✳ Use the back rings of the oven when cooking and turn pan handles inwards, away from the edge of the hob.
✳ Don't use chip pans.
✳ Use short or curly flexes with kettles.
✳ Keep hot drinks and irons away from young children.
✳ Set your hot water temperature lower (no more than 46°C).

## Poisoning

✳ Keep all medicines, alcohol, essential oils, household chemicals and DIY materials out of reach and locked away.

## Drowning

* Always supervise children when they are in or close to water.
* Never leave a child under five alone in a bath.
* Empty the bath immediately after use.
* Cover garden ponds and make sure water butts have lockable lids.

## Cuts

* Fit safety glass in doors/windows and use safety film on glass in furniture.
* Fit safety catches on drawers.
* Keep scissors and razors out of reach.

## Choking

* Supervise young children when they are eating or drinking.
* Keep small objects, such as coins and buttons, away from young children.
* Keep plastic bags and cling film out of reach.
* Follow the age recommendations on toys.

## Accidents outside the home

While under-fives are most likely to have accidents in the home, when your children start school you have a whole new set of circumstances to worry about. Suddenly the outside world becomes a place of potential accidents – the road, the playground, the playing field, other people's houses – it's a wonder that parents let their children out of their sight. But, of course, most mums and dads realize the importance of their children having a life outside the home environment where they will mix with other people and gain life experiences that will help their children become adults.

There are, however, lots of things that you can do as a parent to dramatically reduce the likelihood of your child being involved in an accident outside the home. The statistics may seem frightening, but they do include accidents that happen as a result of parents not taking measures to protect their children from harm.

It seems obvious, but taking precautionary measures will dramatically reduce your child's chances of being in an incident. Take accidents as a result of cycling, for example. In 2003, in the UK, 18 children were killed in cycling road accidents: 577 were seriously injured and just over 4000 children suffered minor injuries. While that may seem like a lot, there are three things to bear in mind. Firstly, that many of the children who were seriously injured or died in these accidents had failed to wear a safety helmet. Research among children who cycle has shown that wearing a helmet reduces the risk of head injury by 63 per cent and the risk of losing consciousness by 86 per cent. In other words, you can actually *alter* your child's chances of being seriously injured by making them wear a safety helmet.

The second thing to consider is that, however frightening it might feel to let your children ride a bike (and there's no doubt that most parents worry about their children when they are out cycling), the long-term health benefits for your child far outweigh any potential risk from an accident. According to the British Medical Association, the gain of 'life years' through improved fitness as a result of regular cycling exceeds the loss of 'life years' in cycle fatalities by a factor of 20 to one. Put another way, obesity and other health problems linked to a lack of exercise are 20 times more likely to kill you than a cycling accident.

The last thing to consider is that, although activities outside the home are often a cause of childhood accidents, this does not mean that children will not get injured if they are kept at home. As the statistics show, children stand an equal chance of being injured in an accident at home as outside it.

## Make your child safe away from home
The best form of accident prevention is to understand what activities your child gets up to away from home. Age plays a large part in what they will be doing, so here's a quick run through of what to expect when, and some relevant safety measures that you can take.

Children under eight should be supervised by an adult at all times when they are outside the home because, although children of this age are beginning to develop common sense, they are still far too young to understand many of the dangers present in the outside world. A great thing to start doing at this age is introducing the idea of potential hazards while making it into a game. That way they will be keen to spot problems before they happen. For example, it's never too early to start teaching the basics of road safety – holding your child's hand at all times,

you can instruct them how to cross roads safely and practice the Green Cross Code when you are out together. (If you are not sure about the basics of road safety yourself, the Government have a fantastic road safety website for children at www.hedgehogs.gov.uk with games and advice.) After a few times you can even let them suggest safe places to cross when you are out and about.

In particular, children under eight shouldn't be allowed to cross the road by themselves, as they are still too young to be able to properly judge the speed and distance of traffic. They are also too small to see or be seen by road users. The same goes for cycling on the road, but that doesn't mean young children can't get lots of practice in the safety of the back garden or the park. However, a cycle helmet should still be worn at all times.

## The Green Cross Code

**1 Think first**
Find the safest place to cross, then stop.

**2 Stop**
Stand on the pavement near the kerb.

**3 Use your eyes and ears**
Look all around for traffic, and listen.

**4 Wait until it's safe to cross**
If traffic is coming, let it pass.

**5 Look and listen**
When it's safe, walk straight across the road.

**6 Arrive alive**
Keep looking and listening for traffic while you cross.

Children at this age also need to understand the dangers of fire and water. If you haven't already done so, take your child along to swimming lessons with a qualified instructor who will teach him or her about water safety.

The period between the ages of seven and 11 is a prime time for road accidents involving children. By this age they will probably be keen to take short distances by themselves, so let your child plan safe routes to school and other short destinations. This will encourage him or her to make decisions and take responsibility for their own safety, and you can help them along by inviting them to talk about what is safe and dangerous on the roads.

At this age, your child might also want to start cycling by themselves. If this is the case, try to get them to take a cycling proficiency course. Their school will probably run one but, if not, your local authority will be able to tell you where the nearest course is being held. It is probably still too early for your child to be cycling on busy roads unsupervised, but you can help them find safe places for cycling, away from traffic, while they build up their road sense. Make sure they are wearing a helmet and reflective clothing at all times.

## ✷ Invest in safety equipment

To help you create a safe environment and eliminate needless risks, invest in basic pieces of child safety equipment, including child locks, fireguards, smoke alarms, cycle helmets, stair gates and pond covers. Remember that certain items of safety gear, such as safety belts and child car seats, are compulsory by law.

## ✷ Teach basic safety

Show your children the ground rules both inside and outside the home, and then let them acquire experience under supervision from a responsible adult.

## ✷ Who they can trust

Encourage your child to be wary of strangers, but also teach them that in an emergency situation, or when lost or scared, they should find someone in uniform to help them out.

## ✷ Keep things in proportion

Don't let worry spoil your experience of being a parent or unnecessarily limit your child's development. Worry about the

# Kris' Top Tips

real risks to your child's safety – such as road traffic, lack of exercise, domestic violence and poor diet – while keeping a sense of proportion about random risks such as murder and abduction.

## ✱ Set a good example

If you want your children to be safety conscious, set a good example both at home and when you are out and about. Lots of parents lecture children about road safety, for example, but then don't follow the basic rules themselves.

## ✱ Get involved with the school

Your child will spend a large proportion of their time away from you at school, so you need to feel reassured that it is a place that takes child safety seriously. Ask about the school's written safety and bullying policies, and encourage them to host child safety courses such as cycling proficiency and the Green Cross Code.

## ✱ Think about your child's personality

Don't underestimate your child's natural tendencies – if he or she has a risk-seeking personality, you will need to channel their energies into positive physical pursuits.

## ✱ Do a first aid course

Even in the safest of environments, children have an uncanny knack of finding danger. If the worst should ever happen, you'll be better prepared if you've taken a child first aid course. Your local surgery should have details of courses near you.

## ✱ Ask where, who and when

Older children will expect some degree of freedom when away from home. To keep them safe, try to ensure that you always know where your child is, who they are with and when they'll be back. Get them to give you a contact telephone number if

they can, or consider getting them a mobile for emergencies.

## ✱ Teach your child 999

If your children get into trouble while away from home, make sure they always know that they can dial 999 in an emergency. There is also a second emergency number, 112. N.B. These numbers should only be used if life is threatened, someone is injured or you suspect that a crime has been committed.

# 10

# Communication

The way we interact with our children makes a huge difference to their happiness and confidence as adults. Communication and emotional intelligence are particularly important. Interacting with your child is about how you communicate with them – and about teaching them these skills that will be so important to them as they grow up.

## Communicating with your child

**The older they get, the more inclined children become to withhold information from their parents – whether it's about practical matters, such as what's happening at school, or emotional issues, such as sex and confidence. The process whereby children gradually tell their parents less about their lives is natural and healthy – it's how they begin to make discoveries and experiment with the independence they acquire.**

**But the word 'experiment' is key here. By definition, experimentation means sometimes not getting it right, and this can occur during the times when children retreat too far away from their parents simply to 'see what happens'. There are things you can do if this situation arises, but the most important thing is to keep calm and accept that it's a natural part of growing up, and they are just seeing how it feels to be self-reliant. If you stay calm and don't overreact to a situation, your children are much more likely to come back to you when they realize your advice and support is valuable and important to them.**

## Emotional Intelligence ('EI')

So what is emotional intelligence? It began as a theory of psychology in the early 1990s, so it's a relatively new concept, but an incredibly important one. Until very recently, psychologists tended to view intelligence strictly in terms of simple abilities such as verbal, numerical and spatial skills. However, this view completely ignored one of the most important aspects of intelligence that humans have – the ability to understand emotions in both ourselves and in others.

So emotional intelligence, put simply, is how good we are at understanding our emotions and those of others, and to what level of subtlety and complexity we do this. For example, most of us can spot when someone is feeling angry, but how many of us can tell when that anger is hiding something else – such as fear, sadness or worry?

The kinds of abilities that would be counted under emotional intelligence are as follows:

### Sensitivity
Awareness of someone else's moods and feelings.

### Understanding
The ability to understand someone else's problems (even if you haven't experienced them yourself), and communicate this to that person.

### Empathy
Being able to put yourself in someone else's shoes.

### Sympathy
Being caring and gentle when someone is upset or troubled.

### Anticipation

Being able to predict how an event or a discussion will affect somebody, based on their personality and experiences.

### Diplomacy

Handling a difficult problem or subject in a way that least upsets somebody else.

### Timing

Being able to judge when it is a good time for someone to hear something difficult or upsetting.

'Normal' intelligence (verbal, numerical, and so on) is something that can be developed through practice, good teaching and exposure to lots of different problems and the methods for solving them. Emotional intelligence is exactly the same – as we broaden our minds, so we can also broaden our EI.

Our EI develops and grows constantly throughout our lives. Infants understand little about emotions, but by the time they're about three they can recognize the most common ones. A big change, of course, occurs during puberty, when children begin to experience lots of totally new emotions that they never knew existed. It's no wonder puberty can be such a difficult and confusing time.

But even into adulthood we are gaining new emotional intelligence as we are exposed to new emotions. Grief, for example, is something that many of us may not fully experience until middle age, when for the first time someone close to us dies. Over the course of that loss, and for months or even years afterwards, we gain some completely new emotional intelligence that wasn't there before.

## Why EI is important for parents

Using emotional intelligence is important right from birth. Parents have to learn very quickly to recognize emotions in their babies – pain, fear and hunger being the obvious ones. When things are going well, of course, other emotions that our babies express, such as contentment and excitement, can bring us great joy and satisfaction.

As babies become toddlers, their 'emotional range' expands – frustration and anger appear, as well as puzzlement and fascination. When toddlers learn to talk, our understanding of our child's emotions is given a big boost, because children will tell us exactly how they're feeling. But as communication is improving, so is the complexity of our children's emotions. With puberty, as we'll see later, come changes that make it hard for children to explain how they're feeling, and even harder for us parents to work it out for ourselves.

## Having confidence in your emotional intelligence

In previous chapters, I've talked about the negative labels we give to ourselves and to our children, and what we are actually capable of. We might say that we weren't very bright at school, or that we're just 'not very sporty', and nine times out of ten these labels are nonsense – they're just a sign that we've never gained confidence in that particular activity.

Emotional intelligence is exactly the same. You often meet people who say they're not very good with emotions, or 'just not very sensitive'. This is simply untrue. Everybody has emotions, everybody has the ability to understand them in others, and everybody has the ability to develop and improve their EI. The only people for whom this isn't the case are those suffering from rare medical conditions such as autism or Asperger's syndrome.

This doesn't necessarily mean that when someone says they're not very good with emotions that it's a cop-out or some kind of emotional laziness. Just like academic performance or sport, early bad experiences or a lack of support from our own parents or loved ones can shake our confidence in an ability and, as with sport or academia, this can cause some people to give up trying to understand others, or be sensitive to or empathize with them.

If you don't have a lot of confidence in your own emotional intelligence, this is something that you will need to address in order to be a successful parent. All children need understanding – it's too important to give up on. But, by the same token, have confidence in your children's emotional intelligence too and don't underestimate their ability to understand complicated emotions. Just as with normal intelligence, the idea should be to constantly 'stretch' your children's emotional understanding. A great number of parents feel it is their duty to protect their children from all emotional upset, but really, the opposite is true. You need to expose your children to emotional issues in such a way that they'll be able to handle them, learn from them and grow stronger as they get older. Children who reach adolescence without any real emotional experience will often suddenly find themselves in emotional situations later on and as a result can struggle to cope.

## Being an emotional role model

This is no less important when it comes to emotional intelligence than for something 'down-to-earth' such as diet or exercise. When children are growing up and struggling to get to grips with their own emotions and those of others, they look to us to help them to understand these feelings, but also to see how to behave in certain situations. For example, young children who see their parents treating others with care and sensitivity are more likely to do the same, whereas children who see their parents dismissing the feelings of others or refusing to engage in conversations about emotions, will do exactly the same.

Being a good emotional role model for your children will teach them vital skills for later life – in work, in relationships, and for when they themselves become parents. In a way, you should see yourself as part of a cycle: the lessons you teach your children now about dealing with feelings are very likely to be copied by them when they have children. It may be that your parents weren't very sensitive or understanding with you, but you have the power to break that cycle, and to teach your children a better way of doing things.

## Understanding your child

Emotional intelligence requires the understanding of certain basic key principles. One of these is the principle that everyone is different – not just in their tastes, interests or academic ability, but in their personalities and temperaments. You can't be emotionally intelligent without using this as a guiding principle for the way in which to conduct relationships with others.

In parenthood, this idea that we're different is crucial. Your children are different from...

### ...You

Although they share your genes, in personality and in temperament children are often very different from either or both parents. They are also growing up in a world that is far removed from the one you grew up in, and this will influence their personalities in a big way.

### ...Their siblings

Variation in personality between siblings is caused by an assortment of things, including birth order and early experiences such as illnesses, unusual talents or disabilities.

### ...Their friends

This sounds obvious enough – after all, there's no reason why two children from different families should have anything in common – but the reasons behind why children choose their particular friends are complex. Sometimes they pick a friend because they are like them, but sometimes it is for the opposite reason – because they are different and therefore interesting. Romantic relationships are just as unpredictable, and we rarely fall in love with someone who is identical to us in every way.

When many parents have their first child they believe that they are a sort of 'blank canvas' and that, with the right parenting, they'll become exactly what the parents would like them to be – clever, confident, well-behaved, and so on. It's usually after the second child arrives that parents realize how much of their children's personalities is 'innate' and not necessarily to do with the environment in which they grow up. Two children raised in exactly the same way will often turn out to be completely different: one might be outgoing, the other shy; one might perform brilliantly at school, whereas the other might find it a struggle.

From your point of view, the important thing is to get to know your child's unique temperament, accept it (rather than try to alter it), and then change the way you deal with them accordingly – especially when they're very young. This principle works for all sorts of things, such as taking your child for their first day at school. If they are confident and sociable, let them run off and play with their friends as soon as they get there; but if they're shy, don't push them away, instead comfort them as much as possible and take time to persuade them why they'll enjoy being at school.

Many parents find this a difficult principle to put into practise because they don't want to be seen to treat their children differently; they worry that if they're inconsistent, one or both children might accuse them of favouritism. The way to deal with this is to explain to them the point that we've made here – that everyone is different, with different needs, personalities and so on.

None of this means that there aren't principles of good parenting that will apply regardless of your child's temperament, but it's how you put those principles into practice with each child that counts.

## Communication

Imagine a teacher in a classroom taking an important lesson with a class of children. Imagine the teacher just sitting there and saying nothing for the whole 45 minutes. The children wouldn't learn much, would they?

Now imagine a second classroom. In this one, the teacher talks almost constantly for the 45 minutes, full of interesting information, speaking in a lively and clear style, but at the end of the lesson the teacher asks the class a question only to find that 90 per cent of the children stopped paying attention long ago. They've learned more than they did in the first classroom, but not much more.

Finally, imagine a third classroom. The teacher in this classroom is also lively and clear, but as well as that, this teacher does something else: he asks questions of the pupils constantly, he listens to what they say, and then he tells them what he thinks. The lesson is more like a discussion than a lecture, and so the pupils learn far more because they feel as though their opinions are important, as well as the teacher's.

## A two-way process

You'll very likely have heard this saying before: that *communication is a two-way process*. It's an idea that the majority of us would agree with, but agreeing with it and putting it into practice are very, very different things. Nowhere in life is practising two-way communication harder than in parenthood – but why is this so?

Parenting is full of pitfalls and traps. In the tough times it can feel as though being a parent is like a test, in which someone is trying to catch you out at every possible opportunity. One of the biggest traps comes from being in a position of authority. Although you have the power (which might feel like a good thing), you also have the responsibility, the hard work, the worry and the guilt, while your children have the happy, fun-filled childhood that you're desperately trying to create for them.

Another common trap parents fall into is *knowing better than your child*. We could talk about the 'wisdom of youth' until the cows came home, but at the end of the day, for their earlier childhood at least, you will have a better idea of how to handle a situation than they will. So, as we all feel from time to time, why bother communicating with our children about how and why something needs to get done? Surely we should just get on and do it as quickly and efficiently as possible? After all, ultimately the final decision will be made by us as parents anyway.

The reason we fall into both of these traps is that we forget the main aim of parenting. It *isn't* to do everything for your child, such as:

* Ferry them round like royalty.
* Protect them from all possible dangers.
* Make sure they get good results at school, even if it means doing the work for them.

The main aim of parenting is *to teach*.

As a parent you are a kind of teacher on a constant basis: this other role involves teaching your children how to interact with others, how to take responsibility, how to overcome difficulties, and so on. In so much of what we do with our children, it's not whether or not the outcome is successful – it's how much they've learned along the way – *and they won't learn anything unless you communicate with them patiently and clearly*.

Let's look at communication from another angle. What *can* be affected if parents don't communicate properly with their children?

## Learning

Parents need to teach their children all sorts of things throughout their lives; from discipline and boundaries, to how to manage their money, and to emotional issues. If you can't communicate with your children, then this learning simply can't take place.

## Mutual understanding

Your understanding of your children, and their understanding of you, depends enormously on regular, clear and open communication. There is so much that you need to know about each other, and this need doesn't lessen the more time you spend together. Parents and children who don't communicate can simply find that they don't know each other at all.

## Trust

It's vital that your children trust you, and this comes in part as a result of your ability to communicate with them: it's very difficult to trust someone if you don't understand what they're saying to you.

## Emotional support

Your children will need your emotional support throughout their lives. They'll need to feel that they can come to you and talk about anything that is bothering them without you dismissing what they say, being impatient because you don't understand, or flying off the handle if they've got themselves into trouble. None of this will be possible unless you can communicate with them.

## Direction

By this we mean 'guidance', and this relates to all sorts of things. Children who stop talking or listening to their parents are the ones who are most likely to get into trouble or stop living up to their potential. They are also the ones who are more likely to feel unloved and insecure, leading to unhappiness and a loss of confidence.

## Listening

The key to successful communication is *listening*, and this is all the more important for people who are in a position of authority. The most successful leaders and managers, and the ones who are most successful at maintaining their authority, are those who really listen to what their staff have to say.

It's just the same for parents, too. You are a leader – the leader of a family – and your children will quickly lose faith in your leadership if they don't feel that you listen to them enough. Many parents tend to think of parenting as an exercise in conveying information and instructions to their children, and these are often the same parents

who complain that their children never tell them anything. But why should they tell us anything if we don't listen to what they have to say?

There's a very simple rule of thumb that you can follow here: in any conversation with a child, you should each be talking for 50 per cent of the time. It doesn't matter whether you know more about something than your child, or if you have started the conversation and it's about something that you have to tell them; you should still be listening for 50 per cent of the time. If you don't listen, you'll have no way of knowing whether they've understood you.

So we know that conversations should be as equal as possible – now for the really important bit. We might have the right intentions and know that we ought to listen, but many parents think this simply means 'letting your child have a say' or, effectively, allowing enough silences in your own speech to allow them to talk. This is important, of course, but it's only a small part of what listening is really about.

Remember: *listening is about taking a genuine interest in what someone is saying*. You could let your child babble away for hours, but unless you're actually listening to what they say, and thinking about it as they say it, it might as well be wasted time.

We all get into conversations with other adults in which we can tell that they're not really interested in what we're saying – whether it's at work, in a shop, or with friends and relatives – but the ability to notice this is not just restricted to adults. Don't forget that from a very early age, children pick up on this too. Don't kid yourself that you can pretend to listen while in fact you're wondering whether you set the video, or thinking about that important meeting tomorrow.

### Did you know?
Three out of four children aged between 11 and 16 say that 'being listened to' is the thing that determines how happy they are about their relationship with their parents.

## Other tips for how to be a good listener

Leave silences in a conversation from time to time – silence gives children the opportunity to talk about something on their own terms. This is often true of really important issues, such as emotional problems.

## Ask open questions

This means questions that can't be answered with a 'yes', 'no' or 'don't know'. Ask questions that require detail and explanations.

## You don't have to agree with everything

The important thing is that you've listened to what your child says, and thought about it. You've shown that you respect them. After that, it's OK to explain why you don't agree with something they've said – as long as you give good reasons.

## Don't stop communicating when things are going well

Good communication is a habit, like keeping a tidy home or eating healthily. You need to keep the habit going all the time and that way, if a problem does arise, your child will find it easier to talk to you.

## Switch off the TV while talking

The same applies to all sorts of distractions, such as doing chores or looking after another child.

Make an effort to give your child your time and your complete attention.

### As often as possible, keep an open mind

You can't always change decisions on your child's say so but, wherever possible, be willing and ready to change a decision if your child gives you genuine reasons as to why you should.

Finally, a quick point about starting conversations. When we get home from work, the last thing we want to talk about is work, so why should children be any different about school? If you're starting a conversation, choose something your child will be interested in. Begin with something that will engage their interest – such as friends or hobbies – it's much easier to talk to a child about something mundane (like schoolwork) once they've already had a fun conversation about music or fashion.

## Communicating with older children

We all know the cliché about teenagers – on the day of their thirteenth birthday they magically transform from angelic, doting cherubs into something resembling a junior member of the Hell's Angels. Disrespectful, messy, disorganized, lazy and – worst of all – uncommunicative. And then, of course, on the morning of their 18th birthday (or as they find their first serious boyfriend or girlfriend – whichever comes first), down they come to breakfast immaculately dressed and spewing forth helpful information like a power shower on full. As they're pouring you a cup of coffee as if it were standard practice, you swear you can see a slight halo round their heads.

Is this cliché about how teens develop really how things are? If you've got teenagers already

you'll have your own ideas, but research suggests that there's at least an element of truth about it, as reported by both teens and their parents.

### Did you know?

Almost half of all teenagers say that they feel unable to discuss problems with their parents. The most common time for these communication problems to appear is between the ages of 12 and 13. The problem tends to be worse for boys than girls, but children of all ages say they are more likely to talk to their mother than their father.

Many parents notice a significant drop in communication with their children some time during the early teens. There are a number of reasons as to why this takes place, but there's one that dwarfs the others – puberty. Here's why puberty has such a strong impact on teenagers and the way they communicate, as well as what you can do to help:

### Physical changes

The physical changes that occur during puberty are genuinely upsetting and strange for many children and in some cases can lead to mild depression and 'cutting off' from others.

Embarrassment can be key here, and this is often misread by parents. So give your children privacy and personal space wherever possible. Offer advice (generally better received from the parent of the same sex), but don't pressure them to take it as this can make things worse rather than better. Finally, teach your children to be proud of

## Exercise **Recalling your own teenager years**

If you have children who are approaching their teens, all these changes might sound frankly terrifying. Well, for children it certainly can be. But, as with many stressful events that we face in our lives, the best thing we can do to stay calm is to familiarize ourselves with what is going to happen, before the event.

Take some time to recall your own teenage years. Do as many of the following as you can over a period of a weeks:

### Memories
Remember everything you can about being a 12–13 year-old – where you were, your friends, your school and your hobbies. Some memories might be more painful than others, but persevere because it will give you valuable insight into what your children are going through.

### Personal items
Schoolbooks, music and old clothes (if you still have them) are great for prompting reminiscences about your teenage life.

### Talk to family and friends
Ask your parents what they remember about your teenage years – everything from your personality to physical changes.

### Speak to other parents
Other parents are great to talk to because they went through their teenage years at a similar time to you, and they may even have teenage children now.

and comfortable with their bodies before they reach their teenage years, and warn them that changes will happen so that it's not a shock when the time comes.

### Romantic and sexual feelings
Like physical changes, new found romantic or sexual feelings can be confusing, scary and embarrassing. The same advice applies here as above – give them space and take the opportunity, if it's presented, to reassure your child that their feelings are natural and healthy. Don't make fun of them under any circumstances.

### Personality changes
The 'split personality' cliché about teenagers does hold true in some cases. Hormonal and physical changes can cause major, unpredictable changes in a child's temperament, personality and moods. It's because the personality is heavily influenced by the chemistry of the brain. This can be extremely puzzling for parents, especially if you yourself had a fairly easy time of it when you were a teenager. As for your child, puberty can create totally new feelings of anxiety, depression, hyperactivity and many other things. Their natural reaction to this can be to cut themselves off for fear of losing control in front of their families or others. The best approach for adults here is to listen, and take whatever your teenagers say about how they're feeling seriously.

You might think that your children are also responsible for communicating, and surely if they cut off from you, that doesn't mean it's your fault... Well, as children get older and have to take responsibility for all sorts of things, they do need to take greater responsibility for communication

# Kris' Top Tips

✱ Develop and have confidence in your own emotional intelligence, even if you don't think understanding and sensitivity are your strong points.

✱ Understanding your child's unique personality is vital, but remember that children's personalities are constantly changing and they may show different sides to themselves when they're not in your company.

✱ Remember what it was like to be a teenager, and how difficult it can be. Use your past experiences to guide how you communicate with your children when they are that age.

✱ If your children 'cut off' from you at any point, there are all sorts of possible reasons. Don't assume the worst, and don't discount the possibility that your child is simply anxious or embarrassed about something.

✱ Communication is a two-way process. Within any one conversation with your child, you should be aiming to talk for 50 per cent of the time and listen for the other 50 per cent – even if you're trying to communicate a set of instructions. If you don't, you wouldn't know whether they've understood you or not. It's harder than it sounds, but don't give up.

✱ Don't forget that parenting isn't just about the end result – it's about what your children learn along the way. They won't learn anything unless you communicate with them constantly.

✱ Parenting isn't about sheltering your children: they should be exposed to emotional events as soon as they are able to understand them. It will give them experience, a sense of responsibility, and strength in the future.

✱ Remember how important it is to be a good role model for your children when it comes to emotions, feelings and communication. The behaviour you're teaching them now will influence them for the rest of their lives.

✱ Talk to other parents and your children's friends and teachers – they can often give you other perspectives and fill in the gaps about things your children aren't telling you.

– with parents, teachers and friends to name just a few. And yes, if your child does cut off from you suddenly (very often in adolescence), it doesn't *necessarily* mean you're to blame, or that you could have seen it coming and prevented it.

There are all sorts of other reasons why children, and particularly adolescents, 'cut off' like this. For some it's a case of exploring independence and emotional distance from their parents, whereas for others it's about enjoying the first experience of privacy. There is, of course, one other sadly common reason, too – bullying.

If you are worried that your child is being bullied, ask them directly. Children are often frightened to talk about what is happening, so be prepared for your child to deny that there is anything wrong at first. Encourage them to talk to you by saying that you are concerned and you want to help and support them, whatever the problem. Take whatever they say seriously, and try to find out exactly what has been going on. Don't promise to keep the bullying secret, but do reassure them that the more they tell you, the more you'll be able to sort out the problem.

**Did you know?**

In 2000, research involving 2,300 pupils aged 10–14 from schools across England found that 30 per cent of children did not tell anyone that they had been bullied. This percentage was higher for boys and older children.

Developing communication skills between parent and child doesn't necessarily have to happen in a contrived way. If neither of you feels comfortable sitting down in an empty room and discussing things, then sometimes it can be helpful to develop communication skills as part of an other activity. This approach is what Kris suggested to the Reynolds family.

Despite the fact that eight-year-old Michael seemed to spend a lot of time with his parents, Alma and Ian, little of that time was spent actually communicating – the TV was the main focus of the family's attention. Alma and Ian clearly doted on their son, but the insular world they created

# Case Study **The Reynolds**

meant Michael was suffering socially as a consequence.

Kris suggested that, to help develop the relationship between father and son, Michael and Ian should spend time away together, by themselves, and go camping. As well as being good fun, the primary motive was to get Michael and Ian communicating in a positive way. By sharing skills including learning how to put up a tent or catch a fish, both father and son could practise expressing emotions such as trust and mutual understanding; both of which are key to good communication.

The camping trip also helped Michael and Ian develop a closer bond and enjoy time together away from any other influences. The results were a great success – both Michael and Ian had a ball and they now make a point of spending regular quality time together.

# Further resources

**BBC websites**
www.bbc.co.uk/bbcthree/tv/killing_
the_kids
www.bbc.co.uk/health
www.bbc.co.uk/parenting

**British Dyslexia Association (BDA)**
Tel: 0118 966 8271
Web: www.bda-dyslexia.org.uk

**Bullying Online**
Web: www.bullying.co.uk

**Child Alert**
Web: www.Childalert.co.uk

**Child Poverty Action Group**
94 White Lion Street
London N1 9PF
Tel: 0207 837 7979
Web: www.cpag.org.uk

**Department of Education**
Tel: 0870 000 2288
Web: www.dfes.gov.uk

**Department of Health**
Tel: 0207 210 4850
Web: www.dh.gov.uk/Home/fs/en

**Department of Transport – Road Safety Advice**
Web: www.hedgehogs.gov.uk

**Dyscalculia**
Web: www.bbc.co.uk/skillswise/
tutors/expertcolumn/dyscalculia

**Feed me Better Campaign: Jamie's School Dinners**
Web: www/feedmebetter.com

**Food Standards Agency**
Tel: 0207 276 8000
Web: www.food.gov.uk

*House of Tiny Tearaways* by Dr Tanya Byron, BBC Books, London 2005

*Little Angels*, by Dr Tanya Byron and Sacha Baveystock, BBC Books, London 2005

**Medical Research Council**
Tel: 0207 636 5422
Web: www.mrc.ac.uk

**National Attention Deficit Disorder Information and Support Service**
Tel: 0208 906 9068
Web: www.addiss.co.uk

**NSPCC**
Tel: 0207 825 2500
Web: www.nspcc.org.uk

**Parents Centre**
Web: www.parentscentre.gov.uk

**Parents Line**
Web: www.parentlineplus.org.uk

**UK Government**
Web: www.direct.gov.uk/Parents

**World Health Organisation**
Web: www.who.int/en/

# Acknowledgements

To my gorgeous three kids who show me what works (and what doesn't!) and my ever patient and loving husband. Also to my mum and dad who taught me everything I know about parenting.

Special thanks to my highly supportive partners at the innovation company ?What If! and everyone who has worked on the programme; and in particular Robin Ashbrook, Dympna Jackson and Elisabeth Bayliffe for taking a chance on me!

Thanks also to Sally and Alistair Bevan, for all their fantastic research and help with the book, and to Emma Shackleton for spotting the potential of the programme and transcribing it into a book to help parents.

BBC Worldwide would like to thank Jon Tonks, Billie-Jo Boyd, Olivia Hall, Nicholas Ivanov, Jordan Smith, Peter Wilding, and James and Joe.

All photographs: Chris Capstick © Pearson Education, with the following exceptions.

Screen grabs: © BBC; p. 15, 24, 28, 32, 34, 41, 42, 45, 49, 70, 86, 89, 110–11, 119, 124, 135, 146, 150, 182–3

Photographs: © BBC; p. 35, 55, 70, 89, 105, 124, 135, 146, 151, 183

Morphs: © BBC; Glassworks 100–1, 140–41

# Index